D1006541

"Having built and sold four successful companies, John knows the secrets to creating a sellable business. John shares his own experiences and lessons learned, and talks about his new book, *Built to Sell*."

E-Myth Worldwide

"What do buyers look for when buying a business, and what should entrepreneurs be doing if they want to sell their firm? If you want to know, I strongly suggest you pick up a copy of *Built to Sell*, by John Warrillow. Covering every important aspect of the process, from attracting multiple bidders to getting the most for your business, this book easily explains what you must know and do if you want to create a business you can sell."

Steve Strauss, *USA Today*

"A terrific boon to all the folks I deal with on a day-to-day basis that are lurching from customer to customer trying to get out of the quagmire. Some terrific lessons which go far beyond my 'How to catch a Leprechaun' chapter in my book which chronicles basically the same observation about the lack of preparedness of most business owners for the sale of their business. One of the strengths of the book is the continuity. It was great following Alex through his trials and tribulations. Very real-life. I fully intend on sharing with my customers and TEC. I'm sure it will be a tremendous success!"

Bruce Hunter, Chair, TEC (Vistage) Canada

"John Warrillow's story gets business leaders to focus on a critical question: If others wouldn't pay a fortune for your business, do you have a business worth growing? This is essential reading for owners looking to build a valuable business."

Verne Harnish, founder, Gazelles, and bestselling author of *The Rockefeller Habits*

"By contrast [to Michael Gerber's book *The Most Successful Small Business in the World*], in *Built to Sell*, Toronto-based serial entrepreneur John Warrillow, a columnist with the *Globe and Mail*'s Your Business section, is much more grounded, focused and effective on how to turn your business into one you can sell. It's a well-told, sensible approach, with lots of tips clearly demarcated within the fable for entrepreneurs to ponder and follow as they dress up their business for sale and then take it through that complicated, delicate process, with millions of dollars at stake."

Harvey Schachter, *Globe and Mail* (Toronto)

"Your business just might be worthless if you don't read this book."

John Jantsch, bestselling author of *Duct Tape Marketing*

"FANTASTIC! Small businesses *need* this book. So many business owners have the dream of building a business that's bigger than themselves, and getting away from the tyranny of constantly putting out fires. John's book is an entertaining, to-the-point way of showing them how to do it. They might just find they like their business much better and not even want to sell later. But if they do sell, they'll get much more value from following the book's advice."

Anita Campbell, editor in chief, *Small Business Trends*

"As we've always advised at StartupNation, the end depends upon the beginning. *Built to Sell*, like other great business books, brings into clarity the game-changing importance of clearly envisioning the destiny of your business. But even more, it tells you how to bring that destiny to life."

Rich Sloan, cofounder and chief startupologist, StartupNation

Built to Sell reminds me of Eliyahu M. Goldratt's *The Goal*, in the way that the valuable lessons about successfully exiting a service business are intertwined with Alex Stapleton's compelling story. Alex's story drew me in immediately. Any current or aspiring service business owner should read *Built to Sell* and take heed of John Warrillow's valuable lessons and Alex Stapleton's enriching and engaging experience."

Mike Handelsman, general manager, Bizbuysell.com

BUILT
TO SELL

BUILT TO SELL

CREATING A BUSINESS THAT
CAN THRIVE WITHOUT YOU

John Warrillow

PORTFOLIO/PENGUIN

PORTFOLIO/PENGUIN

Published by the Penguin Group
Penguin Group (USA) Inc., 375 Hudson Street,
New York, New York 10014, U.S.A.
Penguin Group (Canada), 90 Eglinton Avenue East, Suite 700,
Toronto, Ontario, Canada M4P 2Y3
(a division of Pearson Penguin Canada Inc.)
Penguin Books Ltd, 80 Strand, London WC2R 0RL, England
Penguin Ireland, 25 St Stephen's Green, Dublin 2, Ireland
(a division of Penguin Books Ltd)
Penguin Books Australia Ltd, 250 Camberwell Road, Camberwell,
Victoria 3124, Australia
(a division of Pearson Australia Group Pty Ltd)
Penguin Books India Pvt Ltd, 11 Community Centre, Panchsheel Park,
New Delhi–110 017, India
Penguin Group (NZ), 67 Apollo Drive, Rosedale, North Shore 0632,
New Zealand (a division of Pearson New Zealand Ltd)
Penguin Books (South Africa) (Pty) Ltd, 24 Sturdee Avenue,
Rosebank, Johannesburg 2196, South Africa

Penguin Books Ltd, Registered Offices:
80 Strand, London WC2R 0RL, England

This edition published in 2011 by Portfolio / Penguin,
a member of Penguin Group (USA) Inc.

10   9   8   7   6   5   4   3   2   1

Previously published by Flip Jet Media Inc.

LIBRARY OF CONGRESS CATALOGING IN PUBLICATION DATA
Warrillow, John, date.
    Built to sell : creating a business that can thrive without you / John Warrillow.
      p. cm.
    ISBN 978-1-59184-397-9 (hardback)
  1. Sale of business enterprises. 2. Entrepreneurship. I. Title.
    HD1393.25.W37 2011
    658-dc22   2010049338

Printed in the United States of America
Set in Fairfield Light and Ellington MT
Designed by Sabrina Bowers

Foreword

In almost three decades at *Inc.* magazine—first as senior editor, then executive editor, then editor at large—I have had many great mentors, and they've given me an extraordinary education in entrepreneurship. Among the many things I've learned from them has been the fundamental paradox that lies at the heart of company-building, at least as it is practiced by the smartest entrepreneurs: You should always run a company as if it will last forever, and yet you should also strive constantly to maximize its value, building in the qualities that allow it to be sold at any moment for the highest price buyers are paying for businesses like yours.

That's the philosophy of Jack Stack, the cofounder and CEO of SRC Holdings Corp. in Springfield, Missouri, with whom I have written two books, *The Great Game of Business* and *A Stake in the Outcome*, that explore the mechanisms he and his colleagues have used to create such an enterprise. It's also the philosophy of Norm Brodsky, the serial entrepreneur with whom I have written another book, *Street Smarts* (formerly *The Knack*), as well as a long-running column in *Inc.* of the same name.

And it's the philosophy of John Warrillow. John, in fact, refers to this approach as having an "options strategy," as opposed to an "exit strategy." The idea is to have as many choices in the future as possible. When you follow an options strategy, he says, you build systems and a management team around you so that if a buyer comes along, or you decide it's the right time to get out, you have a sellable business. Or so that you can install a president and move into a chairman's role, which is a kind of quasi-exit. Or so that you can stay involved day to day and work on building an enduring company that can go on without you.

The point is that the best businesses are sellable, and smart businesspeople believe that you should build a company to be sold *even if you have no intention of cashing out or stepping back anytime soon.* If you share that belief, this book is right up your alley. John does a masterful job in *Built to Sell* of illuminating the qualities that business buyers look for in a company, and he does it in a thoroughly enjoyable and engaging manner: by telling a story. Although Alex Stapleton, the lead character in the story, owns an advertising agency, the fundamental lessons he learns apply to any business, and reading about them can only serve to sharpen your thinking about how to make your own company sellable, no matter what type of business you are in.

John is certainly the right person to turn to for advice on this subject. Few people know the world of small business better than he does. I first heard about him in connection with a conference that his business, Warrillow & Co., organized every year to help Fortune 500 marketers figure out how to sell to small companies. The conference had acquired a reputation as the premier event for learning what smaller businesses wanted and how best to reach them. In addition to the conferences, Warrillow & Co. produced in-depth research papers on small business, based on annual surveys of some ten thousand business owners. A hundred giant corporations paid the firm substantial fees for access to those papers, as well as for the insights John and his associates had developed along the way. John himself hosted a nationally syndicated radio show on entrepreneurship. That's actually how he came to start his business: Big companies began approaching him for advice on reaching the small business market. He went on to sell Warrillow

& Co. in 2008, which he couldn't have done without building a company that could continue to thrive without him.

And that's why this book is so good. John Warrillow has studied entrepreneurs; he's interviewed hundreds of them on the radio; he's built his own company around the small business market; and he's sold that business to someone else. If you want to find out what it really takes to build a sellable business, it's always best to listen first to someone who has done it himself. John Warrillow is your man.

Bo Burlingham
Editor at large, *Inc.* magazine and author of
*Small Giants: Companies That Choose to Be
Great Instead of Big*

Preface

This book is about how to create a business that can thrive without you. Once your business can run without you, you'll have a valuable—sellable—asset. I could have written this book as a step-by-step guide, filled with checklists and charts, but instead I chose to tell a story.

This is the story of an imaginary business owner named Alex Stapleton who wants to sell his business (in this case an advertising agency). The business is successful, and Alex has gained a loyal following of customers, but he has a problem. Since he has the most experience in his field, he does most of the selling for his company, and, not surprisingly, Alex's customers all want him to personally oversee their projects.

Stretched thin and running from one fire to the next, Alex reaches a plateau and finds it impossible to get to the next level with his business. When he decides to sell, he meets with his old friend and successful entrepreneur Ted Gordon. The story unfolds as Ted teaches Alex how to turn his business into a sellable company.

While the story is fictional, Alex's experiences are very real for many business owners. There are approximately twenty-three million businesses in the United States, and yet only a few hundred thousand are able to be sold each year. That means for every small business owner who creates a business that someone will buy, there are about a hundred businesses that do not sell. This book provides a framework and action plan for ensuring that you are among that desired 1 percent.

This story is not an autobiography. Alex and Ted are an amalgam of the people I've met and experiences I've had over the fifteen years I have spent covering the small business market. My first exposure to the life of a business owner was as a floundering recent college grad when my parents took me to an awards show celebrating a group of successful entrepreneurs. I listened to their amazing life stories and decided to create a radio program to tell those stories. The radio feature was called "Today's Entrepreneur," and I interviewed a different entrepreneur every weekday for three years. I started an events business and a marketing shop, then spent twelve years building a research company designed to help enterprise companies target small businesses. We interviewed and surveyed more than ten thousand business owners each year in an effort to delve deep inside their heads. I was lucky enough to have had a handful of mentors who collectively make up the sage wisdom embodied in the character of Ted Gordon.

One of the most important things I learned from these mentors was that even though it's sometimes hard to imagine that you'll ever want to leave the company you worked so hard to build, there are many reasons for wanting to build a sellable business:

Your company may be your best shot at a comfortable
    retirement.
You may want to start another business.
You may need cash to deal with a personal financial matter.
You may want more time for yourself.
You may want to sleep better at night knowing that you *could*
    sell your business if you wanted to or needed to.

Of course, this is just a sampling, but no matter what is motivating you to create a business that could be sold, I hope you find the story of Alex and Ted inspiring and helpful.

Please stay in touch by joining the community of business owners who are creating businesses that can thrive without them at www. BuiltToSell.com.

John Warrillow
Twitter: @JohnWarrillow
Facebook.com/BuiltToSell
Weekly blog updates: BuiltToSell.com/blog

Acknowledgments

They say that it takes a village to raise a child. I feel the same way about writing a book. This project is the sum total of what I have learned in business from starting and ultimately exiting four businesses. My first business was a flop and I probably would have stopped there had it not been for the help, encouragement, and guidance of an incredible set of mentors. Ted Matthews combines Richard Branson's marketing savvy with Mother Teresa's heart. Thank you, Ted. Other teachers include Michael de Pencier, David Drew, Jay Gordon, Bruce MacLellan, Louise Mitchell, Rob Paterson, Dan Sullivan, and Dan Taylor (1952–2009).

Bo Burlingham is one of many authors who gave their time and talent. Other authors who helped with inspiration and advice include Jim Blasigame, Anita Campbell, Tom Deans, John Ellett, Jason Fried, Seth Godin, Verne Harnish, John Brown, Shep Hyken, John Jantsch, Rich Sloan, Tim Ferriss, Gary Vaynerchuk, Guy Kawasaki, Bob Bury, Doug Tatum, Ken Blanchard, Norm Brodsky, Chris Brogan, Chris Guillebeau, Jeremy Gutsche, Tom Peters, Jonathan Field, Dan Pink, Gretchen Rubin, Marshall Goldsmith, and Pamela Slim.

My editors Matt Quinn and Mike Hofman at *Inc.*, Sean Stanleigh at the *Globe and Mail*, and Lindsay Blakely at CBS Interactive sharpened my thinking.

Andrea Nickel and Perry Miele at Beringer Capital taught me about the mysterious world of mergers and acquisitions. Beringer is a boutique firm that punches well above its weight. Other smart people I leaned on for advice on the mechanics of doing a deal include Randy Cochran, Ron Dersch, Ritch and Mike Epstein, Michael Henry, Diane Neiderman, Steve Parrish, George Rossolatos, Rob Slee, and Colin Walker.

Carol Franco acted as my agent and confidant.

A handful of small business market thought leaders encouraged this project, including Doug Case at Wells Fargo, Elisa Cool and Evan Blank at the *Wall Street Journal*, Steve Chadwick at Verizon Wireless, Kareem Chouli at VISA, Barry Ellison at BDC, Glauco Ferrari and Cindy Bates at Microsoft, Walter Good and Wendy Vinson at E-Myth Worldwide, Mike Handelsman at BizBuySell.com, Deborah Herman at SunTrust, Beth Horowitz at Discover Network, Bob Lapointe at *Inc.* magazine, Shane Lawrence at TD, Randy McCollum at Administaff, Kyle McNamara and Dave Wilton at Scotiabank, Jeff Parker at US Bank, Bruno Perreault at MasterCard, Derrick Ragland and Stephen Miller at HSBC, Karen Ripperger at The Principal, Karen Sawyer and James Wong at BMO, Karen Larrimer at PNC, Susan Sobbott, Howard Grosfield, and Denise Pickett at American Express, and Keith Williams and Becky Roemen at Entrepreneurs' Organization (EO).

My EO forum mates Mike Boydell, Sam Ifergan, Steve Horst, Sean Hunt, Joe Stutzman, and Dean Tai shared a lifetime of business and personal experiences with me.

Thank you to the team at Portfolio, most importantly my editor Brooke Carey.

Cathy Witlox has a sharp eye that I could not write without.

I tortured many friends by forcing them to read early drafts and concepts for this book. To Rich Cooper, Liane Hunt, Simon Tuplin, and Trevor Currie, thank you for seeing through the typos and making this a better book.

Thanks to my sister Emma (she's the smart one), who taught

me that there is a difference between wanting to sell a business and wanting to create a sellable business.

Mom, thanks for encouraging me to read and write even though I couldn't stand doing either when I was young. Thanks for teaching me to count to ten backward before a big speech and for being the very first copy editor of this book. Dad, you taught me everything I know about business and being a father and I'll always try to be half as good as you were at both.

To JB and The Lads, you make it all worthwhile.

Contents

Foreword   vii

Preface   xi

Acknowledgements   1

1 A Company in Chaos   9

2 A Worthless Business?   19

3 Putting the Process into Practice   27

4 Pressure from Within

5 The Test   36

6 The Candidates   44

7 Growing Pains   52

8 The Number   64

9 Gaining Momentum   70

10 A Blank Check for Growth   82

11 Telling Management   90

12 The Question   97

13 A Sellable Company   104

14 The Finish Line   110

Implementation Guide: How to Create a Business
  That Can Thrive Without You   115

Summary of Ted's Tips   147

Recommended Reading and Resources   151

BUILT
TO SELL

1   A Company in Chaos

lex Stapleton wheeled the Range Rover into the parking lot of MNY Bank. He grabbed his portfolio from the backseat and sprinted to the doors. A quick check of his watch made it official: 9:06 a.m. He was late—again.

As a regular visitor, Alex's name was on the list at reception, and the security guard waved him in. He found an open elevator and hit the button for the eighteenth floor. He took his first full breath of air since leaving his office.

As soon as the doors opened, Alex sprinted down the hallway and straight into the boardroom where he always conducted meetings at MNY Bank. His client, John Stevens, was waiting for him, looking testy. "Sorry I'm late, John. Traffic was crazy for a Friday and—"

"Did you bring the mock-ups?" John asked impatiently.

John had worked at the bank for seven years. He'd landed a job as an account manager straight out of business school and spent a few years lending money to small businesses before getting a job in marketing at the bank's head office. Pudgy and prematurely bald, he seemed angry at life, and even though he had no formal training in marketing, he insisted on directing every detail of Alex's work.

Alex unzipped his portfolio, wiped his brow, and settled in for the long haul. He unveiled the first design and John didn't flinch, waving Alex off the moment he began to explain the designer's vision for the piece.

"Let's see the next one."

After Alex presented all eight concepts—several weeks' work condensed to less than thirty minutes—John took his time before selecting a design and then gave his instructions. He wanted another illustration, the font changed, and the red to be more orange-red instead of the pink-red selected by Alex's designer. John droned on with more feedback, and Alex felt as if he were back in elementary school. Despite being woefully unqualified, John seemed to relish his new role as art critic. Alex left the meeting room promising John another round of mock-ups by Monday morning. He pulled out of the parking lot feeling broken.

———•———

If John Stevens had been an atypical client, Alex could have lived with it. Unfortunately, John represented the bulk of Alex's clients: marketing managers with crappy jobs who seemed to like pushing around their marketing agency.

Alex had started the Stapleton Agency eight years before, after moving up the ladder at a multinational marketing agency. Once he'd gotten as much out of that job as he felt he could, he decided he needed a new challenge and ventured out on his own. He started out designing logos and brochures for small businesses and gradually moved up to becoming an approved vendor for MNY Bank. Having approved vendor status meant that the bank paid their bills and kept the Stapleton Agency on a short list of alternative suppliers to their agency of record. When the bank's main marketing agency rejected smaller jobs, the bank summoned the Stapleton Agency.

When Alex started the agency, he dreamed of working on important campaigns with large budgets. He imagined directing models and actors between booze-soaked lunches with chief marketing officers. He wanted to be part of the scene. Instead, he was trying to figure out how to explain to his designer that she would need to work through the weekend because the client—a middle manager who had never taken a design course, doing a job he was completely unqualified for—insisted on what amounted to a design overhaul.

———•◦•———

The Stapleton Agency was located in a funky part of the city just west of downtown. Alex paid $4,000 a month for more space than he needed with the hope that it would impress clients. The office had all of the requisite touches befitting a creative shop: exposed brick walls, glass-encased boardroom, twelve-foot-long boardroom table, and a permanently mounted overhead projector. Sadly, it rarely served its purpose—MNY Bank insisted that Alex come to them.

Upon returning to the office, Alex tried to slip into his office without his senior designer, Sarah Buckner, noticing, but she heard his keys jangle. She looked up from her computer.

"How'd it go?"

"Pretty good. He had a few changes, but nothing major. I'll come see you in a few minutes."

With that, Alex went into his office and shut the door. He needed caffeine. The day's mail was on his desk and he quickly scanned it for the familiar blue-and-gold logo of MNY Bank. He was expecting a check.

Alex collected his thoughts and prioritized the next few hours. He needed to get Sarah working on the MNY Bank changes, go across town for lunch, get back to write a proposal, and find time to call his banker.

Sarah rolled her eyes as Alex delivered the news. He knew how hard Sarah had worked on this project—and how much she'd hated doing it—so he tried to present John's instructions in a way that wouldn't squash her motivation. She accepted her sentence, donned her sound-canceling earphones to shut out the sorry world she found herself in, and set out to find the proper shade of orange-red that would appease Lord Stevens.

Alex kicked himself for not standing up to John. He felt weak, but the reality was the Stapleton Agency could not afford to lose MNY Bank as a client. Last month, the bank amounted to $48,000 of the Stapleton Agency's $120,000 in total billings. Alex, Sarah, and the other six employees of the Stapleton Agency needed MNY Bank.

———•———

Traffic was heavy on the way across town and Alex was late for his second meeting of the day. Sandy Garmalo sat at the table sipping San Pellegrino. She ran the marketing department for a law firm and had been Alex's client for five years. The law firm never generated huge billings for the Stapleton Agency, but they were steady, which meant Alex had to spring for lunch once a quarter. For Sandy, Alex's lunches were a nice escape from the overbearing lawyers she served.

The waiter arrived and asked if they would like a drink. Alex was about to ask for a Diet Coke when Sandy preempted him.

"I'll have a glass of your house white."

Alex had too much to do that afternoon but knew that letting Sandy drink alone would make lunch awkward.

"I'll have the same," he said, promising himself that he would nurse one glass.

Sandy was a divorced fifty-something woman, ten years older than Alex. She enjoyed flirting with him, and Alex obliged, knowing that a little harmless amusement would keep the projects flowing.

Appetizers were picked at. More wine arrived. As Sandy rambled on about the lawyers she worked for, Alex became increasingly disinterested. Eventually, the waiter cleared the plates and dessert was offered and refused. Sandy requested a coffee. Resigning himself to another ten minutes of meaningless banter, he ordered an espresso.

The bill came and Alex produced his credit card. One of the perks of owning the Stapleton Agency was the ability to charge $8,000 worth of expenses per month on his card, which generated a nice stash of travel points that he promised himself he'd use this year to take his wife and two kids on a vacation. Alex sat nervously as the waiter went away, and he asked the credit gods for a little bit of understanding. He'd been late paying off his balance last month and was cut off until his account was back in good standing. His bill was due again sometime this week and he hoped the date had not passed.

The waiter returned. The card had snuck under the watchful eyes of the bank's credit department. Alex smiled, retrieved the card, signed the receipt, and got on with the business of extracting himself from lunch. Sandy made some vague overtures about upcoming projects she would need the Stapleton Agency's help with. Alex feigned interest and eventually made his escape.

After grabbing yet another coffee en route, Alex returned to the office to work on the proposal he'd promised to tackle that afternoon. The request for proposal had come in from Urban Sports Warehouse (USW), a local sporting goods retailer. They had grown tired of their agency and were looking for a new marketing firm to handle all of their work, which included newspaper ads, local radio spots, store banners, and an e-commerce-enabled Web site.

Alex knew that his team could handle the print ads and in-store signage. He had a friend at a production house who could help with the radio work. Most of the Web site work would be outsourced, but USW didn't need to know that.

After pasting the requisite drivel about the history of his agency, its creative credentials and awards, Alex began to estimate his fees. There would be hard costs for studio time, proofs, and freelance Web designers. Then he tried to estimate the staff's time. He billed his designers at $200 per hour and his own time at

$300 per hour. These were largely arbitrary rates established over time by researching how much competitors charged.

Alex hated the process of estimating hours. He knew it was an inexact science and that his actual hours invested would have no resemblance to what he was estimating. Creating marketing material was such an iterative process that there was no way to estimate his time accurately.

After four hours of writing and doing some fuzzy math, the proposal was done. It was 6:30 p.m. and he had missed the FedEx guy for the day, so he dropped the proposal off at the depot on the way home. He handed it to the clerk and hoped that USW would be the client that would finally make him less reliant on MNY Bank and the likes of John Stevens.

Alex decided it was safe to call Mary Pradham's office, given the late hour and knowing that she usually left early to get home to her kids. Mary was his account manager at MNY Bank, which had required him to move his business banking there after he made it onto the bank's approved vendor list. Alex was bumping up against his $150,000 line of credit, and by steering clear of a live conversation with Mary, he could avoid another one of her cash flow lectures. Ironically, he'd been expecting a check from Mary's employer today, but it hadn't arrived.

Alex left Mary a voice mail explaining that he'd pay down his line of credit as soon as he received the anticipated check. He hoped that would buy him a few days. The Stapleton Agency provided him with a decent income and a great vehicle for tax write-offs. He ran the Range Rover through the business and was sure to keep the bill whenever he ate out with friends. He had been able to give himself a bonus of $150,000 last year on top of his $100,000 annual salary. Not bad, but the cash flow was lumpy, and this wasn't his first after-hours call to Mary.

———•———

Alex spent a good deal of his Saturday in the office under the guise of catching up on paperwork—which did need to be done.

But his main reason for sending his wife and kids shopping without him while he returned to the office was so he could be on hand to supervise Sarah's work. She was his best designer, but she hadn't heard John Stevens's criticisms firsthand. He had. By the time the two of them left that afternoon, he felt Sarah had everything under control and would be able to finish up rather quickly on Sunday.

On Monday morning, Alex met for breakfast with an old client who owned a local car dealership, so it was after 10:00 a.m. by the time he got to his office. As soon as he arrived, he knew it was going to be a bad day. Taped to his door was a note from Sarah:

Sunday, 4:00 p.m.

Alex:
We need to talk.

Sarah

This was not going to be good. He'd hired Sarah away from a rival agency last year. He needed her for all of the MNY Bank work. Resigned, he walked over to her desk.

She looked up from her work. "Let's do this in your office."

Sarah followed him back to his office and closed the door. She didn't waste any time.

"Look, Alex, I like you and the rest of the team here, but I'm going back to my old job at Curve Designs. I'll wrap up the brochure project for MNY, but when that's done, I'm out."

Alex felt rejected. He knew that there was nothing he could say or do. Working the weekend to revise the MNY Bank brochure to accommodate a client who knew nothing about design had finally pushed Sarah over the edge.

The meeting ended with Alex making some weak attempts to thank her for her service. Both knew the damage was done, and neither wanted to be where they were at that moment. Sarah went back to her earphones and computer. Alex sat back in his chair and considered the rest of his team.

Leveling with himself, Alex knew that he had assembled a mediocre staff. Sarah was the best of the lot. He had two other designers who were generalists. They could create decent brochures, functional Web sites, and acceptable print ads. Neither of them excelled at any one discipline. His account directors were equally average. Before joining the Stapleton Agency, Dean Richardson had been an account supervisor at a large local agency. Having been passed over twice for promotion to account director, he had been easy prey for Alex to recruit with an offer of becoming an account director at the Stapleton Agency. Alex knew titles were a currency he could afford to be liberal with.

Rhina Sullivan was the other account director at the Stapleton Agency. She was efficient and detail-oriented. However, as account director, she was also responsible for client strategy, which was over her head.

Despite Dean and Rhina (or perhaps because of them), all of the Stapleton Agency's clients wanted to deal with the boss. Alex's name was on the door, so he needed to attend virtually all client meetings. Losing Sarah meant his other designers would need to work overtime. He'd need to rely on Dean and Rhina to handle more clients while he spent time recruiting a new designer. His team, average to begin with, would be stretched to their limits.

When he started his agency, Alex had dreamt of attracting the best talent in the city, paying them well, building a magical work environment, and eventually selling out to a multinational agency holding company. In reality, he had second-rate generalists working at the beck and call of ignorant clients. It wasn't supposed to be like this.

Alex was tired of the grind and decided it was time to sell his company.

2   A Worthless Business?

Ted Gordon had been a family friend for decades and had inspired Alex to become an entrepreneur. Ted had built and sold a number of businesses over the years and Alex had watched him reach new heights of personal and financial freedom.

Ted was a serial entrepreneur. He had made his first million starting, and ultimately selling, an insurance agency. He had moved on to build a consulting company, which he sold to a global firm. He had also sold a commercial real estate business a few years earlier. By the age of fifty-nine, Ted had started, built, and sold four businesses. His net worth was well into eight figures. And not only was Ted a success in business, he was also a success in life. He had been married for twenty-six years and had two adult kids who still talked to him. There were also annual ski trips and long summers at the beach house. It seemed like Ted had figured things out, so Alex decided to give him a call.

"Hi, Ted. It's Alex."

"Hey, Alex. How are you?"

"I'm okay. Would you mind if I came up to see you? I'd like to get your advice on something I've been contemplating."

Ted's office was on the top floor of a building downtown that overlooked the water. When Alex arrived, a receptionist informed him that Ted would be right out. A few minutes later, Ted came out of his office and put an arm around Alex.

"So, I see you've met Cindy. Did she offer you a drink?"

"She did, and I'm fine, thanks."

They walked into Ted's office, which had a panoramic, unobstructed view of the water. The office was large—probably a thousand square feet—adorned with pictures of Ted's family and a hefty oak desk that Alex imagined had been the epicenter of many deals.

They shunned the desk for a more comfortable spot on two white leather chairs divided by a glass coffee table. Ted rested his feet on the coffee table.

"Why did you want to see me?"

Alex knew that he could confide in Ted, so he got to the point. "I've decided I want to sell my business."

"That's a big decision, Alex. Let's back up a minute, what made you decide to sell?"

Alex recounted the story of MNY Bank, Sarah and the rest of his mediocre team, and the company's lumpy cash flow. He talked about how clients always wanted to deal with Alex himself and his agency's dependency on MNY Bank. Ted listened carefully, asking questions for clarification.

After about thirty minutes, Ted asked a question that seemed somewhat odd. "How would you describe your business to a stranger at a cocktail party?"

Alex thought about this, slightly aggravated to be answering a question Ted knew the answer to already.

"We're a marketing agency. We create marketing materials like brochures, print ads, and Web sites."

"Who's your competition?"

Alex launched into the list of marketing agencies in town. "There are other small shops like Reynolds & Harper, Fuel, and Curve Designs. Sometimes we lose out to regional offices of large agencies. There are a lot of freelancers who work from home and—"

"So you run a service business highly dependent on a small group of important clients who in turn demand that you personally tend to their account, and you compete with a lot of other players who provide similar services."

"You could put it that way."

Ted paused a minute before offering his valuation analysis. "Alex, your business is virtually worthless today."

Alex couldn't believe what he was hearing. He'd spent eight years building the Stapleton Agency, and now the man he most respected in life and in business proclaimed it worthless.

"Are you saying I can't sell my business?"

"No, I'm saying that you can't sell it *today*. If you want to sell it, we need to work on making some changes in your business. I can help, but it won't be easy. You'll need to make some tough decisions and bold changes. Are you prepared to follow my advice?"

"Yes."

"Let's meet here every Tuesday morning at 9:00. In the meantime, I want you to go away and think about what kind of projects you're really good at. Come back next week and we'll talk about what's involved in selling your business."

On his way home, Alex opened his mobile phone and checked his e-mail. John Stevens had seen the latest round of revisions and had more changes to make to the brochure.

———— • ————

Back at the office, Alex took an inventory of projects that needed to get done for the week. In addition to finding a way to placate John Stevens, the Stapleton Agency needed to design and print the *Free Checking* branch posters for MNY's retail banking group; redo a Web site for the largest BMW dealership in town; optimize the Web site of a local bike shop to improve its natural search ratings; design a logo for a new software company; and write a direct mail package for MNY's credit card division. It would be a busy week and Alex needed extra effort from each of his employees.

Before he was able to panic too much, Alex forced himself to confront the first task of the day—reviewing the most recent draft of a direct mail letter his only copywriter, Tony Martino, had created for MNY Bank's new travel rewards credit card. Tony was by all accounts a mediocre writer, but he had chosen a career in advertising because he thought it would make him more attractive to the opposite sex. He had been in the bottom half of his class at college, and upon graduation had bounced around five agencies over three years. On his résumé, Tony characterized his long stretches of unemployment as "freelancing," which was a charitable interpretation of his time spent toggling between video games and online poker. Somehow, Tony had managed to land a short stint at a respected agency in town, so eight months ago, when Alex was desperate for a copywriter, he hired Tony after a thirty-minute interview.

Now Alex regretted his haste. Tony's most recent copy was a string of bad clichés held together with spelling and grammatical errors despite the fact that it was his third draft. Alex drew a large black line diagonally across the page and scribbled *REWRITE* at the top. He tossed the page to the side of his desk and promised himself to get rid of Tony as soon as he could replace Sarah.

Since Sarah had been preoccupied with the project for John Stevens, Alex had put his youngest designer, Elijah Kaplan, in charge of the *Free Checking* branch posters. Elijah came in to show Alex's his designs, and even though Alex thought they might be a little too edgy for the bank's taste, he was relieved that they were done. He sent Elijah to have the posters proofed and printed in the morning. That left Chris Sawchuk as the only designer to work on the Web site for Buddy's BMW and the optimization project for the bike store. Chris was reasonably savvy with Web sites but by no means a specialist. Through some reworking of copy and tags, he had managed to get the bike store ranked fourth among Google natural searches for road bikes and fifth for bike service. The client wanted to be first or second in both categories. Chris broke the news to Alex.

"I can't get them above the fold. I've tried all of my usual tricks and they're still only coming up fourth."

Alex resigned himself to another difficult conversation with a client.

———•———

Elijah was the son of a marketing manager at MNY Bank, so Alex had been inclined to hire him six months ago. Word had circulated among the design team that Sarah was leaving, and Elijah spotted his opportunity.

"Hey, Alex, do you have a minute?"

"Sure, Elijah, come on in."

Elijah walked into Alex's office and closed the door behind him.

"I've been here six months now and we're stretched pretty thin these days. I've been logging some late nights and I think it's time I get a little bump in my salary."

Alex started counting under his breath so as not to explode. Because Elijah's mother worked at MNY Bank, he was given a starting salary that was 10 percent higher than was typical for a junior designer. Alex was furious that this little brat had used Sarah's resignation to ask for a raise when he knew full well Alex couldn't refuse.

Choosing his words carefully, Alex said, "What do you have in mind, Elijah?"

"I think a $5,000 raise would get me to where my peers from design school are. It seems fair under the circumstances."

Alex decided to buy himself some time.

"Elijah, you're a key member of the team and I appreciate the extra work you've been putting in lately. Let's set up a meeting next week where we can sit down for an hour and talk about your progress over the past six months. I'll consider your request and will have an answer when we meet next week."

Elijah, sensing he had his prey on the ropes, agreed.

The following Tuesday, Ted greeted Alex warmly and offered him the same leather chair beside the coffee table.

"So how was your week?" Ted asked.

"Brutal," admitted Alex. "My best designer is leaving, I need to find a writer who can write copy for a credit card campaign, a Web guy who can decode Google's black box, and my youngest designer wants a raise despite being barely qualified to create a branch poster."

"Sounds like you had a tough week," Ted said. "Did you give some thought to the question I asked you last week?"

Alex had spent time thinking about the types of projects the Stapleton Agency was really good at. He had started by sifting through a file of thank-you letters and testimonials from clients. He looked at the time sheets his designers submitted and tracked them back to his most profitable projects. He also thought about the disaster projects over the last year and made a list of the ones that had caused the most problems.

"It seems the work we're best at is designing logos. We have a system we follow every time we get asked to create a product logo. Clients like the work we produce and we're able to charge a good dollar because clients know a product logo is something they will use for a long time. Once we create one product logo, we have our foot in the door and clients often come back as they launch new products."

Ted considered Alex's conclusion. "Tell me about the system you follow for creating logos."

"It's nothing too formal, but we always start off by asking the client to describe their vision for their product and how they differentiate themselves from their competitors."

Ted began to make notes. "That sounds like a good first step. Let's call it Visioning."

Step 1: Visioning

"What's the next step?" asked Ted.

"After we establish the client's goals, we go through an exercise where we ask the client to personify their product. For example, we'll ask questions like, 'If your product was a famous actor, who would it be?' and 'If your product was a rock star, who would it be?' One of our favorite questions is a little goofy: 'If your product was a cookie, what kind of cookie would it be?' These questions force the client to think about the personality they want to come through in their logo."

"That sounds unique, Alex. Let's call that step two and give it a name like Personification."

Step 2: Personification

"What's your next step in designing a logo?"

"We then go back to the office and use a pencil and paper to freehand sketch a bunch of ideas. We'll use the business the client is in along with their vision and the personification exercise to come up with a few icons that represent their product."

"Why don't you use a computer for this step?"

"We've found that if you use a computer to show a client rough drafts, they tend to focus on small details they don't like instead of judging the concepts. So by showing them concepts in rough, we force them to focus on high-level ideas instead of details like colors or fonts."

"Let's call this step Sketch Concepts."

Ted updated his notes with the following:

Step 3: Sketch Concepts

"The client will usually like one of the sketches, which then acts as our basis for creating a version on the computer. Again, we limit the variables a client can see by only designing in black and white. That way the client judges the logo on its design merits before we get into colors."

"I've never heard of a design shop doing that—very smart." Ted added a fourth step to his notes:

Step 4: Black-and-White Proofs

"Once clients like what they see in black and white, we show them color options and they select one. After they select colors, we provide the client with digital files and a brand standard guidebook, and then our work is done."

Ted updated his sheet with the final step in Alex's process:

Step 5: Final Design

"It sounds like you have a five-step logo design process."

Ted angled his notebook so Alex could see what he had written:

Step 1: Visioning
Step 2: Personification
Step 3: Sketch Concepts
Step 4: Black-and-White Proofs
Step 5: Final Design

Alex took in Ted's notes and was surprised to see the process they had been following unconsciously for some time suddenly appear on paper.

"What if you focused your business on just doing logos with the Five-Step Logo Design Process?" Ted asked.

Alex immediately recoiled. "There's no way we could build a business on just logos! MNY Bank doesn't even use us much for their product logos, and they represent 40 percent of our business today. Plus, our other clients think of us as their agency and we get asked to do all sorts of projects for them."

"That's the problem, Alex. You're accepting too many different projects, so you need all kinds of different talent on your team. You're a small shop, so you have to hire generalists who are inevitably not as good as the specialists the big agencies can hire. So you're asking generalists to perform specialists' work and the results are weak."

TED'S TIP #1

Don't generalize; specialize. If you focus on doing one thing well and hire specialists in that area, the quality of your work will improve and you will stand out among your competitors.

"But if we just do logos, we'll have to stop working for MNY Bank."

"Alex, relying on MNY provides you with some cash flow, but it's going to make it very difficult to sell your firm. Nobody wants to buy a business where 40 percent of the revenue comes from one company. It's too risky. If you want to sell your business, you should have a diverse group of clients where no one company makes up more than 10 to 15 percent of your revenue."

TED'S TIP #2

Relying too heavily on one client is risky and will turn off potential buyers. Make sure that no one client makes up more than 15 percent of your revenue.

Alex contemplated this advice for a moment and asked for clarification. "So what exactly are you suggesting, Ted?"

"In each business I've sold, we created a standard service offering, a consistent process for delivering our product or service. We made sure the product or service was something clients would need on a regular basis so we could count on recurring revenue. I'm suggesting you become the world's best logo design shop. Write down your five-step process and start talking to prospects about your standard service offering. I'm not asking you to fire your other clients just yet. Start using the Five-Step Logo Design Process with new prospects. Create a one-page description of your approach to creating logos and find ten people to pitch it to. Come back next week and tell me how you made out."

3 Putting the Process into Practice

lex scanned the mail—still no check from MNY Bank. He closed his office door and considered his cash position. The Stapleton Agency had a payroll of $43,000 per month and monthly rent of $4,000. He could put off his other suppliers, but he needed to come up with at least $47,000 by month's end. He glanced at his list of receivables and saw there was $68,000 that was sixty to ninety days in arrears. Along with some small clients who were paying slowly, Alex saw one $52,000 unpaid invoice issued to MNY Bank sixty-five days ago. The bank usually paid in sixty days. They weren't terribly late, but Alex's margin for error was slim. Since MNY Bank was his largest client, he didn't like to pester them about collections, but he knew he couldn't wait any longer.

Alex's e-mail to Ralph Stone in the strategic sourcing department of MNY Bank was brief and cordial, and he hoped it would prove fruitful.

> Hi Ralph:
> I hope you're well. I'm inquiring to ensure you received invoice #12-673 in the amount of $52,000. If you have a moment, could you please drop me a note to confirm it's being processed?
> Thanks in advance,
>
> Alex

Alex hoped for a speedy response.

———•———

Having done what he could think of to improve cash flow, Alex mulled over his recent conversation with Ted and his outline for the Five-Step Logo Design Process. He had five days to visit ten prospects. He quickly mocked up a one-page sell sheet and had Chris lay it out and print ten color copies.

Alex reviewed the Stapleton Agency's Christmas card list and highlighted names he had not spoken with in some time. He fired off two dozen e-mails and hoped to get at least ten meetings to pitch his new process.

———•———

Alex's first two meetings were somewhat awkward as he refined his pitch. His third meeting of the week was with Ziggy Epstein. Ziggy owned Natural Foods Inc., an organic food company that made specialty yogurt and cheese in small batches. Her company supplied most of the specialty food stores in the surrounding area and had used the Stapleton Agency to build a Web site a few years ago.

Alex met Ziggy at a small office attached to her production facility on the outskirts of town. After getting the pleasantries out of the way, he got down to business.

"So, Ziggy, tell me about the new products you're working on."

"We're launching a lowfat version of our yogurt and we're really excited about a new line of organic ice cream we want to launch in the spring."

"The ice cream line sounds like a great extension of your business. Have you come up with a name?"

"Natural Treats Organic Ice Cream."

"That's a great name. Do you have a logo for Natural Treats?"

"Not yet."

Alex spotted his opportunity and launched into his pitch for the Five-Step Logo Design Process.

"Ziggy, it has been a while since we built your Web site.

Including you and your team, we've had the opportunity to work with some great clients over the years. Recently, I did an assessment of all of the projects we've done and came to the conclusion that we're very good at creating logos, so we've decided to specialize. We've developed a five-step process for designing logos and have achieved some great results for clients."

With that, Alex revealed his one-page sell sheet and took Ziggy through the process he had mapped out with Ted's help.

"This sounds like a great process," said Ziggy. "I'd love you guys to work on a logo for our new line of ice cream. Can you send me a proposal?"

⬦

Alex got back to his office, energized by Ziggy's reaction to the Five-Step Logo Design Process, and sat down to write a proposal. Having explained the methodology to Ziggy in person, he only needed to come up with a price tag. Alex started by estimating the number of hours it would take. He looked through the old dockets of logo design projects and estimated that the process, with some back-and-forth for Ziggy's approvals, would take eight to twelve weeks and generate thirty-five billable hours for the Stapleton Agency.

Instead of putting his hourly rates in the proposal, Alex decided that since the project was so well defined, he would gamble and set the price for the Five-Step Logo Design Process at a flat rate of $10,000. The fee was a combination of what he thought a logo was worth, how much agency time it would take, and gut feeling. There was nothing scientific about it.

He e-mailed the estimate to Ziggy and crossed his fingers.

⬦

By the end of Friday, Alex had met with six past clients to pitch the five-step process. He was summarizing his findings when he heard the familiar ping of an incoming e-mail. It was a note from Ziggy.

Alex:

    Thanks for such a speedy turnaround on the estimate.
We'd like to proceed with your proposal. I've attached
a signed copy of your estimate as a PDF. Let me know
when you'd like to meet for Step 1!

    Regards,

                          Ziggy Epstein

Alex pumped his fist and smiled broadly. He had his first client for his new process.

Alex took a celebratory walk around the block. He was basking in the glow of his new assignment when he looked down at his mobile—a missed call. Mary Pradham was trying to reach him.

⊰ · ⊱

After getting the formalities out of the way, Ted wanted the numbers.

"So how did you make out?"

Alex recounted the results of his test of the Five-Step Logo Design Process. He had sent twenty-four e-mails to dormant clients, which resulted in six meetings and one sale to Ziggy.

"Congratulations, Alex, that's great stuff! How did it feel to be talking about your Five-Step Logo Design Process?"

Alex contemplated Ted's question for a minute.

"I felt a lot more confident. In the past when I was pitching the Stapleton Agency I felt like I was groveling for table scraps. We didn't specialize in anything, so I would take any project they would throw my way."

"And how was pitching the Five-Step Logo Design Process different?"

"When I was pitching our process, I felt like I was an expert. I was in control. I felt confident that we have something of value, and I think that confidence was contagious for Ziggy."

Ted smiled. "Good. That's the way it's supposed to feel when you own a product that you control. Alex, I want you to stop thinking of the Stapleton Agency as a service company and start thinking like a product company."

TED'S TIP #3

Owning a process makes it easier to pitch and puts you in control. Be clear about what you're selling, and potential customers will be more likely to buy your product.

"But designing logos is still a service."

"Fair enough, but your product is your unique methodology for designing a logo. A service company is simply a collection of people with a specific expertise who offer their services to the marketplace. Good service companies have some unique approaches and talented people. But as long as they customize their approach to solving client problems, there is no scale to the business and its operations are contingent on people. When people are the main assets of the business—and they can come and go every night—the business will not be worth very much."

Alex pushed back. "But I've heard of a lot of service company founders who have sold their business."

Ted, sounding more impassioned than at any other point in their meetings to date, stood his ground.

"When a service company is sold, the owners typically get some money up front and the rest of their money is contingent on hitting performance goals in the years ahead. It's called an earn-out, and often the owners need to stay on for three years or more to get their money. During those three years, a lot can happen that makes it difficult for the owners to meet the acquiring company's performance goals."

Alex was surprised to see such intensity coming from Ted and needed to know more.

"Why are you so against earn-outs?"

"In an earn-out, you put a significant amount of what your company is worth at risk. The acquiring company is now in control. An earn-out is almost always a disappointment for an entrepreneur. You've assumed most of the risk and the acquiring company gets most of the reward if you're successful. Acquiring companies use an earn-out formula to buy a business when they know the founders *are* the business. Your job is to build the Stapleton Agency up to a point where the business is independent of Alex Stapleton. That's the only way you can sell without putting a lot of your compensation at risk in an earn-out. Alex, you need to train people to handle each of the five steps of your process so you don't have to be the guy piecing every project together from scratch."

TED'S TIP #4

Don't become synonymous with your company. If buyers aren't confident that your business can run without you in charge, they won't make their best offer.

Then Ted said, "Alex, it looks like something is on your mind. Tell me what's bothering you."

"I'm committed to transforming my company into something sellable and I love the Five-Step Logo Design Process, but right now my most immediate concern is cash. I'm expecting a big check from the bank and they're a little late."

Alex's concerns seemed like music to Ted's ears.

"That's another reason to think of your Five-Step Logo Design Process as a product. When you have a product, people expect to pay for it in advance. When you go to Costco to buy toilet paper, don't you have to pay for it before you use it? We're used to paying for products up front and services after they have been rendered. Think about the last time you had your windows cleaned. The service was performed first and then you paid the bill. Products are paid for before you use them. Now that your service has been productized, you need to start charging up front for it."

"I do expect to pay for products up front. If I turn the sell sheet into a brochure and put our fee on the brochure, it would look even more like a tangible product."

Ted brought the conversation back full circle.

"When someone buys a company, they look at the amount of capital they need to tie up to buy the business. If your business is a cash suck—and it sounds like it is right now—then they will be willing to pay less for the business. If your business generates cash, they will be willing to pay more to buy your business. Alex, give me a rundown on how you bill for your service today."

"Once an estimate is approved, we get to work on the project. Once we complete the project, we send our bill and wait sixty days or so for a check."

"And how long does a typical project last?"

"That depends on the job, but a logo project usually takes eight to twelve weeks."

"Alex, I need you to listen very carefully to what I'm about to say. You have a negative cash flow cycle. On a typical logo design project, it takes four to five months before you get paid because it takes two to three months to do the work and another two months before your invoice is paid. The more projects you sell, the more cash you sop up. No wonder your bank is on your case. Now compare your existing cash flow cycle with a model that allows you to charge in advance. You win the project and you ask to be paid before they experience the product. You then get to use their money for two to three months while you're doing the work. Now imagine that you convince five or ten clients to go through the Five-Step Logo Design Process. Now you have $50,000 or $100,000 of your clients' money to finance your business."

Alex, thinking of the possibilities, smiled for the first time in the meeting.

"The more we sell, the more cash we accumulate. I'll never have to grovel to Mary Pradham again."

"And an acquirer will look at your business as a cash generator instead of a cash suck."

Ted offered his instructions for the week.

"Alex, see how many more clients you can get a meeting with to pitch your Five-Step Logo Design Process. This time, make sure you include the price on the sell sheet and the words 'Billed upon signing letter of agreement.' This is your product and you get to decide how it's billed."

TED'S TIP #5

Avoid the cash suck. Once you've standardized your service, charge up front or use progress billing to create a positive cash flow cycle.

Alex left Ted's office feeling confident. He knew if he could start getting clients to pay up front, he would get Mary off his case and sleep a lot better at night.

4 Pressure from Within

Tony clutched his latest draft of the direct mail piece for MNY Bank as if he were choking it. Alex knew the word *REWRITE* with a diagonal line through his work without further explanation would set Tony off.

"Alex, I need a little more direction if you expect me to be able to write another draft," Tony said.

Alex was at a loss for constructive criticism; he didn't know where to start. It wasn't the opening paragraph or the salutation or the P.S. or the offer or the tone or the grammar or the spelling. It was everything about the letter that he found unbearable. Quite simply, Alex was paralyzed by Tony's incompetence.

"Look, Tony, I don't have time for this right now. The bank is all over me for their branch posters and I haven't seen Elijah yet this morning. Let's talk about this later."

Tony rolled his eyes and stalked back to his desk.

Alex checked in with Sarah to see how she was progressing on what he hoped would be the final changes to John Stevens's brochure project. As he approached Sarah from behind, he had a full view of what was on her twenty-one-inch monitor. Instead of the MNY Bank brochure, it seemed Sarah was engrossed in a last-minute travel site.

Alex approached and stood beside Sarah until she noticed him and sheepishly removed her earphones.

"Planning a vacation, are we?" Alex asked, the words dripping with sarcasm.

"Alex, I just—"

Alex raised his hand like a police officer stopping traffic and walked away without waiting for what he knew would be a feeble excuse.

———•———

The mail came in and Alex hungrily opened the white number 10 envelopes. There were three invoices from suppliers and two checks. The checks were from small jobs totaling just over $23,000. Better than nothing, but Alex still needed another $24,000 to cover payroll and rent by month's end. He was now down to twelve business days.

———•———

Alex scheduled his meeting with Elijah for 8:00 a.m.

Elijah walked into Alex's office sporting a smug grin. "Good morning, Alex. How was your night?"

The meeting unfolded as Alex anticipated. Between his mother's job at MNY Bank and Sarah's resignation, Elijah squeezed Alex for a raise. Alex countered with Elijah's age and relative inexperience. The result was a split decision with Elijah getting a $2,500 raise and Alex promising to review his salary again in six months.

Elijah didn't know it yet, but he would not be working for the Stapleton Agency in six months.

———•———

Alex scanned his e-mails and saw the usual client fires. The bike shop wanted a discount on the search engine optimization project because the Stapleton Agency couldn't deliver first or second ranking for their keywords of choice; Buddy's BMW was getting criticism from a lawyer in Munich because their Web site didn't adhere to BMW's brand standards; and MNY's retail banking group wanted another six branch posters printed by the end of the day. Ralph Stone also needed invoice number 12-673 resubmitted with the correct purchase order number listed.

There was an e-mail from Ziggy. She'd enjoyed the Natural Treats personification exercise and was keenly awaiting the sketches as part of step three in Alex's system.

Ziggy's note prompted Alex to put aside the fires in his inbox and turn his attention to developing a new list of prospects to whom he could pitch the Five-Step Logo Design Process.

———◆———

As Alex expected, Ted wanted to start their meeting with a recap of last week's numbers.

"I had eight meetings and Spring Valley Homes agreed to a logo for their new condominium project on the spot."

"That's great progress, Alex."

"In addition to selling a logo to Spring Valley, I also had a good conversation with an old client who asked me for a proposal for a new ad campaign. It would be radio and newspaper ads and possibly a local TV spot."

Ted's face did not reveal his disappointment. "If you win the new advertising project, when will you receive the cash from the client?"

Alex pondered this for a moment. "I think the work will take six weeks to produce, and this client pays quickly, so I should get paid within thirty days."

"So it'll take you roughly seventy-five days from the day you win the project until the day you get paid?" Ted asked, pausing long enough for the ramifications to sink in.

Alex's enthusiasm waned.

"How much time will you have to commit to writing the proposal?" Ted asked.

"It'll probably take me the better part of an afternoon."

"And if you win the assignment, who will work on the print ads?"

Alex pondered this for a moment. Sarah would be gone by the time the work came in. Elijah was too junior, and Chris would be busy with the logos they were already committed to designing. Before Alex could come up with a response, Ted interrupted.

"Look, Alex, if you're going to commit to creating a business that can be sold, you need to commit to offering one process. That means you need to stop accepting other projects."

"But they asked if I would be interested, and we could really use the money . . ."

"Clients will test your resolve every day. They're used to bossing their service providers around and, if given the choice, would always prefer you customize your solution just for them. If you want to sell your business, you can't give in. You'll be swimming upstream. Clients will never know you're serious about specialization until you say no to other work. You can't be 'kind of' a specialist. If you're going to be the world's best logo design shop, you can't also sneak in a few ad campaigns. It's why heart surgeons don't set broken ankles."

Alex continued to resist. "But I'm not in much of a position to be turning down work these days."

"An amazing thing will happen when you start turning down other projects in favor of promoting your specialized logo design process—you'll instantly become more referable. If you offer a generic service like advertising or marketing, people will have trouble describing to their friends why you're special because you are just like everyone else. If, however, you are the world's best logo creators, you'll be memorable and referable. For every advertising project you turn down, you will win a logo assignment."

TED'S TIP #6

Don't be afraid to say no to projects. Prove that you're serious about specialization by turning down work that falls outside your area of expertise. The more people you say no to, the more referrals you'll get to people who need your product or service.

Alex capitulated. "I'll trust you on this, Ted."

"Good, because the next step is important. As we've discussed, the only way to sell the Stapleton Agency is to make it run without you calling all the shots. That means you need to provide instructions to your employees so that they can implement the Five-Step Logo Design Process."

"Are you talking about some sort of instruction manual?" Alex asked.

"Exactly. Imagine your Five-Step Logo Design Process is an assembly line with five machines and you need to teach someone to operate each machine. Start with how to turn it on, how to make it go, and how to read all of the buttons and gauges as it runs."

Listening, Alex started to jot down notes.

"Take each step in the process and write a detailed instruction manual for completing that step. Give the instructions to one of your team members and see if they can follow the directions. Edit it until someone can follow the instructions without you hovering over them. This week, I'd like you to write an instruction manual for the Five-Step Logo Design Process. Bring it with you next time we meet and we can talk about how it is working."

———◆———

The mail was perched precariously on the corner of Alex's desk. He carefully gathered the pile, cradling it close to his chest so as not to lose anything. One by one, he placed the envelopes into two piles. The first pile was for junk mail. The second pile contained white number 10 envelopes. The first pile began to grow: a computer flyer, a conference brochure. The second pile started to grow too.

Once he finished sorting the mail, Alex carefully organized the second pile. He took his letter opener, inserted it into the crack at the top of an envelope, and sliced it open. It revealed an invoice from a photographer they had used for the MNY brochure. The next one contained a $3,400 check, and the next, another invoice. The fourth envelope had MNY Bank's familiar blue-and-gold logo in the top left-hand corner. Alex's pulse quickened. This could only mean one of two things: Either he had received a statement of his accounts from Mary Pradham, or the check had arrived. He inserted the letter opener and made a clean incision. With the envelope fully opened he could see inside. It was a check for $52,000.

———◆———

With the check deposited, Alex felt like he could finally breathe again. He sat down with his cup of Grande Bold and wrote down the instructions he wanted followed for each of the five steps in his logo design process.

For step one, he wrote the exact questions he wanted to ask clients. For step two, he outlined the personification examples to use in such painstaking detail that his eighty-three-year-old mother could administer the questionnaire. For step three, he specified how many sketches to render and what elements of a client's business to use as inspiration for the imagery in a logo. The fourth step included strict instructions on how to present each black-and-white version, including the paper stock to use for printing. The fifth step outlined the detailed color combinations to use and what to include in the style guide given to each client.

By 6:00 p.m., Alex had created a first draft of his instruction manual. It was a complete summary of his vision and directions for creating a logo. Now if he could get his staff to follow the instructions, he could extricate himself from personally overseeing each new logo project.

He went home exhilarated by the thought of starting to build some scale into his business.

———•———

Alex was slightly nervous as all seven of his employees found a seat at the boardroom table. He looked around and sized up his audience. His account directors were sitting next to each other, Rhina attentively with a notepad and sharpened pencil placed neatly in front of her, and Dean beside her, fiddling with his BlackBerry and pretending he had important clients to get back to. The designers were clustered together on one side of the table, with Sarah looking uninterested, Chris thumbing his mobile, and Elijah chatting with Tony. Even Alex's office manager, Olga Retzich, had been asked to attend this important meeting.

Alex started the meeting by setting the stage for the changes he was about to implement. He talked about examples of companies that specialize in one thing. He explained why Southwest Airlines only uses the Boeing 737 model of airplane so that their crew can learn one piece of equipment and maintenance teams can quickly spot problems with one set of diagnostic routines to follow. Alex was proud of his example and used it as a springboard into revealing the changes that were afoot at the Stapleton Agency.

He read a thank-you letter from a client who had used the firm to create a product logo. He also talked about how much more satisfied their logo design clients were when compared to clients overall and how often logo clients returned for multiple product logos over time. Alex admitted where they had gotten in over their heads in taking on advertising projects that went beyond their capabilities.

He used a PowerPoint flowchart to reveal the Five-Step Logo Design Process and talked about the work they were doing with Ziggy at Natural Foods. He passed around a copy of the instruction manual that detailed the procedure for each step.

The presentation lasted forty-five minutes, and then Alex paused for questions. Rhina was the first to speak.

"I like the idea of specializing in something and getting really good at it."

Chris added, "I'd love to do more freehand sketch work. I haven't done any drawing since art school."

Elijah wasn't so enthusiastic. "Specialization sounds great, but I thought advertising was supposed to be creative. What you're talking about sounds like working in a factory."

Dean chimed in. "I think we should be the trusted marketing adviser for all of our clients. How am I supposed to build a trusting relationship with my clients if all I am doing is flogging one service?"

Sarah, with nothing to lose, said, "As a designer, I don't want to be pigeonholed into having to follow a set of rules."

Elijah had triggered a mutiny. Alex felt his temper rising. He inhaled deeply, counted to five, and said, "Our new process still allows plenty of latitude for creativity."

With that, he asked each employee to study the manual and to see him with questions. He quickly adjourned the meeting.

Alex stared as Elijah fumbled to collect his things, refusing to make eye contact with his boss. Anticipating a confrontation, the other employees left the boardroom quickly. Alex walked across the room to close the door.

"Have a seat," he said, pointing to a chair.

Sitting back down, Elijah said, "Alex, I didn't mean to—"

Alex cut him off. "Why did you become a designer?"

"I was always creative as a kid. I like drawing and did well in art class. It just seemed like a good choice."

Elijah might well have gotten high marks in art class, but as far as Alex had seen, his talents didn't translate well to marketing. "Being creative is a great asset," he said, "but the Stapleton Agency is a business. And as a business, our first priority is to make money. If you want to be an artist and have free rein, I suggest you go find somewhere else to work."

"But Alex, an agency is supposed to be a creative environment."

"An agency is a business first. And here, we're focusing on creating logos using our five-step process."

Elijah sat motionless for more than a minute. Resigning himself to the obvious, he said, "Well, I guess I'm leaving, then."

"Good luck."

With that, they shook hands and Elijah returned to his desk. He put a few things in his bag and left.

Alex felt good to have exercised his power as the owner of his own company. After all, his name was on the door and he would not stand for such blatant contempt—especially from his most junior employee. But then the broader implications of what he had just done started to wash over him. He'd be down to one designer. Elijah's mother would find out, and that could jeopardize his relationship with MNY Bank.

A knock on the door jolted Alex out of his fog. It was Rhina.

"Alex, I know the meeting didn't go as well as you had hoped, but I want you to know I'm really excited about our new focus."

"Thanks, Rhina," Alex said, feeling buoyed by her statement. "I think your skills will be well suited for our new process."

5   The Test

lex spent the weekend with Pam and the kids and felt refreshed arriving at the office Monday. He bid good morning to the only employee who'd arrived before him, Rhina, and then settled in behind his desk, turned on his computer, and took a sip of coffee as it fired up.

He scanned his e-mail inbox and noted a message from Blair Donaldson. Alex immediately recognized the name as that of USW's chief marketing officer. The subject line read simply: *Congratulations*.

As he opened the note, Alex's mind began to race. He scanned the first few paragraphs and realized the Stapleton Agency had been offered a contract to become the agency of record for USW.

───────◆───────

Alex decided to do the twenty-minute walk instead of the five-minute drive to Ted's office for their regular Tuesday meeting. It had been twenty-four hours since he received the e-mail from Blair Donaldson, and he needed the exercise to work off the competing messages flying through his brain.

Kicking off the conversation, Alex explained the USW background to Ted.

"I know what you're going to say, but this is a huge opportunity for us. It would mean $50,000 per month in steady fees over the next year."

Alex went on to explain the prestige of being the agency of record for a big brand like USW. He talked about the awards they could win given USW's appetite for creative advertising. Ted didn't interrupt; he wanted to give Alex some time to get all his feelings on the table.

Once Alex finished, Ted said, "Alex, why did you come to me for advice on your business in the first place?"

"Because I want to sell my business. Becoming USW's agency of record will help that effort tremendously. A lot of the big agencies bid for USW, so they'll want to gobble us up to get at their business."

"Alex, if you want to work for a big agency for the next five years, then yes, I think accepting the USW engagement could help you sell your company. But the only way a big agency will buy another small, undifferentiated agency will be if they tie you into a five-year earn-out agreement. They'll offer you a little bit of cash up front and the rest will be contingent on you achieving milestones they set out for you over the next five years. You'll need to keep and grow the MNY account and hang on to USW for the next five years. You'll be answering to a middle manager at a big agency with a lot of rules and procedures of their own. If you miss your targets, they won't be obliged to pay you any more than the small amount of cash you got when you entered into the agreement. You'll be taking all of the risk and will not control the outcome."

Alex contemplated this and wondered if Elijah had already told his mother that her agency had just fired her son.

"My advice continues to be about creating a business that can exist without you. That's the only way to sell your company and be able to walk away without being obliged to stick around for five years."

Ted sensed his protégé needed a pep talk.

"You're doing well so far, Alex. You've identified a service that your firm is good at delivering and you've mapped out a repeatable process for delivering it. You've created an instruction manual so others can deliver the service, and you're charging up front so that the more you sell, the more cash you will accumulate. I told you your resolve would be tested throughout this process. This is one of those moments. I'm not going to tell you what to do about USW. It's your call."

Alex left Ted's office feeling uneasy. He understood Ted's advice intellectually, but he had aspired to win a client like USW for years. He'd worked so hard on his response to their request for a proposal that it was hard to imagine turning it down.

———◆———

Alex reached Blair Donaldson's assistant. She informed him that Mr. Donaldson was finishing a meeting, but that she'd have him call Alex afterward. The minutes felt like hours as Alex waited. Finally, Blair returned his call.

"Mr. Donaldson, thanks for calling back."

"Alex, it's good to hear from you. I'm surprised you didn't call yesterday. We're going to have fun working with you and your team."

"Thanks but . . ." Alex hesitated, summoned his courage, and proceeded. "I have to decline the assignment."

"What are you talking about?"

"Since submitting our proposal to you, we've decided to specialize in creating logos."

"Excuse me?"

"I realized my agency is much too small to generalize. We could never give you our best work if we had to do it all, and logos are our strong suit. I still hope you'll consider us in the future if you ever need a new logo design."

The explanation didn't help.

"You're a fool," Blair said. "You have a tiny agency and we would have made you guys. You better get used to doing business cards for real estate agents, because that's the only work you're going to get in this town after I get through telling the members of the AMA about the time you've wasted."

Alex tried to smooth things over. "I didn't mean to offend you."
The line went dead. Blair had hung up.

———◆———

Alex returned to the office as Dean was preparing to leave for a client meeting. Keen to take his mind off of Blair Donaldson and USW, he struck up a conversation.

"Hey, Dean. Off to see the Spring Valley Homes guys?"

"Yup. We're in good shape. We did the personification thing with them last week and I'm going over there right now to show them some concepts."

"Great, mind if I take a look?" Alex asked innocently as he gestured to Dean's zipped portfolio.

"Sure, I guess," Dean said halfheartedly. He left the portfolio closed and started to fumble as he hurried to put on his jacket. "I'm a little late, but I can give you a quick summary. When we got into the personification exercise, it was clear that they have a big vision for this condo project. They want to sell fifty-six units this fall and make it the first of five condo projects around the city."

"That's great," Alex said, somewhat impatiently. "Can I see the sketches for the logo?"

Dean slowly unzipped his portfolio. "Instead of just showing them sketches, we decided to show them a little bit more of our creativity." He opened the portfolio to reveal a full-color, computer-generated mock-up of a launch campaign. There was a mock-up for a print ad, a brochure, and six logo concepts all printed in full color.

Alex couldn't believe his eyes. "Dean, where did you get the idea to create this material?"

"I think it's a big opportunity for us, and they could turn into a major client."

"Dean, we're focused on logos now."

"Oh sure, I know, and I'm presenting six logo concepts as well and—"

"Yes, I see that and I also see that the logos are full-color,

computer-generated logos, not the black-and-white sketches that
follow the personification exercise in our process."

"But Alex, this is a really big client and I just thought it was
worth going the extra mile for them."

Alex sighed. "I understand." After all, he'd been tempted to do
the same with USW. "But we specialize in logos now and that's all
we do. You need to get your head around the fact that we're no longer an agency. Remove the print ad and brochure mock-ups. You
can still show them the logo concepts, but next time, please follow
the process and show them black-and-white sketches first."

Dean rolled his eyes and removed the print ad and brochure
mock-ups from his portfolio.

———•———

As they approached their regular seats, Alex gave Ted the news.

"I turned down the USW assignment."

"You made a good decision."

"I hope so. USW would have been a big client for us."

Ted, sensing a need to restart Alex's enthusiasm for their work
together, decided to explain the way they were going to replace and
exceed the revenue the Stapleton Agency would have received from
USW.

"To sell your business, you need to demonstrate to a buyer that
you have a sales engine that will produce predictable, recurring
revenue. We need to figure out how many sales reps you need to
drive your sales engine and how many companies are in your target market. For now, let's focus on businesses within the city limits. How many companies are there in town?"

Alex had no idea, so they went to Ted's desk and huddled
around his computer. They found a U.S. Census Bureau Web site
that showed there were 210,000 businesses within a hundred-mile
radius.

Ted wanted to tighten the target market as much as possible.
"Let's assume that to be willing to spend $10,000 on a logo for a

new product or division, a business needs to generate at least $1 million in annual revenue."

Alex scanned the site and found the number. "There are 58,000 businesses in the area that do at least $1 million a year."

"Now we need to know how many of those 58,000 companies you can sell a logo to. Think back to when you started selling your Five-Step Logo Design Process. How many companies did you e-mail?"

Alex did the quick math and produced the number.

"I e-mailed forty-four companies."

"And how many of those gave you an appointment?"

"Fourteen."

"And how many logos did you sell?"

"Two so far."

Ted grabbed a pad of paper and scribbled some numbers. He angled the pad so Alex could see his math.

"Your close rate on prospects is two of forty-four, or 4.5 percent. Let's discount that by at least 50 percent because you had a preexisting relationship with those leads. So let's say your close rate on cold leads is roughly 2 percent. That means the approximate market potential for the Five-Step Logo Design Process is roughly 2 percent of 58,000, or 1,160 logos. That assumes one logo per company, which is conservative given that most companies create logos for new divisions and products on a regular basis. At $10,000 per logo, that's $11.6 million in market potential here in town. That's a nice little business, and we're not even counting how big you could grow if you opened offices in other cities. Nationwide, the business of creating logos could be a $100 million opportunity if you could replicate your model elsewhere."

For the first time in the meeting, Alex started to feel better about turning down USW.

"Not only is an acquirer going to want to know how big your business could become," Ted continued, "they will also want to know that you have a predictable sales formula that allows you to estimate how many sales you can make. For example, you started with forty-four leads, and after two weeks you made two sales. That's one logo for each week you were selling. If the average salesperson has fifty productive weeks per year, each salesperson you hire should be able to sell fifty logos. From there we can project out various scenarios. For example, if you want to achieve $1 million in revenue next year, then you need two salespeople. If you think you can handle $2 million in revenue, or design two hundred logos, then you need four salespeople."

TED'S TIP #7

Take some time to figure out how many pipeline prospects will likely lead to sales. This number will become essential when you go to sell because it allows the buyer to estimate the size of the market opportunity.

"An acquiring company will want to see the model for your sales engine, including how many opportunities you have and your historical close rate, to estimate the market potential. You need to demonstrate you know your sales engine and that you can predict, with a fair degree of accuracy, how your sales engine will perform under their roof. Most importantly, you need to demonstrate that you're not the only one who can sell logos."

"But I don't have any sales reps," Alex reminded Ted.

"I know. You need to hire at least two."

"Why two? Shouldn't I start with one?"

"Salespeople are competitive and they will compete with each other, which will allow you to prove that your sales engine is not just dependent on one good sales rep. Besides, you have payroll and rent that amounts to roughly $600,000 per year, so you need to sell at least $1 million of logos this year to cover your costs and show some profit."

TED'S TIP #8

Two sales reps are always better than one. Often competitive types, sales reps will try to outdo each other. And having two on staff will prove to a buyer that you have a scalable sales model, not just one good sales rep.

Alex started doing the math and it didn't add up.

"If I hire two sales reps, won't my payroll and rent add up to more like $700,000 or $800,000?"

"Yes, if you keep all of the staff that you have now. Spend some time this week thinking about the team you need to administer the Five-Step Logo Design Process. I bet you'll find one or two staff members that you no longer need."

As Alex left Ted's office, he knew he was in for some difficult conversations in the coming week.

6　The Candidates

Firing Tony Martino was an easy decision—Tony was a bad writer to begin with and Alex didn't need a copywriter to administer the Five-Step Logo Design Process. He could always use freelancers for the odd copywriting job the bank handed down. The conversation was quick. Tony was expecting it and Alex treated him fairly.

The conversation with Dean was a little more difficult. Alex tried to soften the blow by describing the strategic projects Dean could work on at a larger agency and how many of his talents would go unused at the *new* Stapleton Agency. Dean left in a huff.

Shedding Tony and Dean saved the Stapleton Agency $125,000 a year. Alex decided not to immediately replace Sarah, which saved the firm another $70,000 per year. He'd found enough cuts to hire two intermediate salespeople without increasing his overall cost base.

———◆———

Blake Worthington had returned from two weeks at his family's summer house. He wore a blue suit over his six-foot-two-inch frame. His crisp white shirt was held together at the sleeves by gold cufflinks, which clinked against a Rolex his father had given him upon graduation from the Cheshire Preparatory Academy. White teeth created the perfect contrast to the golden tan he had cultivated over the fortnight away. His Windsor knot was carefully assembled and his full head of blond hair had been molded into place.

Blake was one of four candidates Alex had short-listed for the newly created sales roles at the Stapleton Agency. They shook hands and started with some easy banter.

Alex scanned Blake's résumé. After Cheshire, Blake had attended Cornell. After graduation, there was a six-month trip to Southeast Asia, where he had learned to kite surf, after which he returned to the United States and took his current job. For the past two years he had served as a junior member of the business development team at one of the big advertising agency conglomerates.

"Why do you want to work for the Stapleton Agency?"

"A big agency is a great placed to be trained, but I want to start seeing the direct results of my work." Blake was obviously telling Alex what he thought he wanted to hear.

"How do you like the advertising business so far?"

Blake sat up in his chair, clearly sensing an opportunity to impress Alex.

"I love the power of a brand. I like understanding the core attributes of a brand and finding a way to express those creatively through a variety of different media. I'm a huge believer in integration. They say TV is dead, but if you want to build a brand you can't beat the reach of TV."

The interview unfolded predictably, with Alex lobbing softball questions and Blake hitting them out of the park with impressive-sounding responses he had probably read in some career advice book but nevertheless delivered convincingly. It ended with Alex promising to be in touch the following week.

Alex was impressed with Blake's polish, pedigree, and big agency experience and thought he would represent the Stapleton Agency well. He put a large check mark on Blake's résumé and filed it with the other candidates still in the running.

Back at his desk, the usual fires were smoldering in his inbox. John Stevens wanted to meet with him tomorrow to go over a Spanish version of the brochure. Olga wanted to know if she could renew the lease on the photocopier. Sarah wanted a reconciliation of the vacation pay she was owed. Then Alex saw Ziggy's name with the subject header *Thanks*. He opened the note and read it:

> Alex:
>
>   I want to let you know how happy we are with the logo your team created for Natural Treats. I just met with Rhina this morning and she took me through the color versions of Chris's design. It looks good and I have already distributed your brand standard guidebook to all of our staff. Rhina was very efficient and moved the project along well. Chris is a creative guy and a pleasure to work with. I'll know who to call for our next product launch. Thanks again,
>
>   Ziggy Epstein

Alex was ecstatic. It always felt good to get a thank-you letter from a client, but typically the letters praised Alex personally for his creativity and thoughtfulness. Ziggy's letter was special because it recognized his team. For the first time, Alex felt like he was building a business that was more than just Alex Stapleton.

Based on Rhina and Chris's work on the Natural Treats logo, Alex put them in charge of the Five-Step Logo Design Process. Rhina would conduct step one, the visioning exercise, and step two, the personification interviews. Chris would be responsible for step three, the sketch, and the computer-generated renditions of steps four and five. Rhina would write and present the brand standard guidebook and manage the client throughout the process. Alex had a system and people to oversee its delivery. Now all he needed was a sales team.

Angie Thacker dressed conservatively for her interview with Alex. Her hair was pulled back and fell neatly over the shoulders of her dark blue suit.

Alex reviewed her résumé. After college at a state school, Angie had landed a job selling mobile phones at a local wireless retailer. She'd been the top salesperson at the store, and after two years selling phones, she had taken a job selling yellow pages advertising for one of the big phone companies. She had quickly risen to be among the top 10 percent of sales reps nationally.

"Why do you want to work for the Stapleton Agency?"

"I love selling and I understand you're just starting a sales team at the Stapleton Agency. I'd love to help you build a professional sales team from the ground up."

"What makes a salesperson professional?"

"The key to my success in sales has always been working my numbers. I know how many meetings I need to close a sale. I know how many sales I need to hit my quota for the week and how that rolls up to help me make my month, my quarter, and my year. It all starts with knowing how many meetings I need to schedule each week and it flows from there."

Alex couldn't believe how scientifically Angie had broken down her goal setting. Intrigued, he wanted to know more.

"What motivates you, Angie?"

"I'm a competitor. I love to win."

The interview continued with Alex feeling like he was at the zoo peering at an exotic animal. Growing up in the creative business, he had always been around creative people. He'd never met anyone so disciplined or with such a linear thought process.

Alex said good-bye to Angie with a promise to respond with a decision next week.

———— • ————

Tuesday morning, Ted called Alex on his mobile to see if he wanted to go for a sail and have their talk on the boat instead of Ted's office. The forecast called for a fifteen- to twenty-knot onshore wind. They agreed to meet at Ted's yacht club.

Although he could afford a much larger vessel, Ted loved the thrill of sailing a small boat on big water, so he had opted for a Laser 4000. Helping Ted rig the boat, Alex outlined his progress since they'd last met. He described how he had made room on his payroll for two salespeople by letting Tony and Dean go and not replacing Sarah. He also described the candidates he was interviewing for the sales roles. He spent the majority of the time contrasting Blake and Angie. Both had left a positive impression on him for different reasons, and he tried to articulate that for Ted.

"Blake understands service businesses. He's worked for an agency for two years and knows the creative world. He understands selling intangibles."

Ted listened intently while hoisting the sails and making his way out of the harbor. While looking at the direction of the wind, he kept probing Alex.

"Tell me about Angie."

"Angie is completely different. She knows nothing about the marketing industry and has spent most of her career selling tangible products that a prospect can touch and feel. Angie is all process and systems and she is extremely goal oriented."

Ted probed further. "Sounds like you have two very different candidates. How about the rest of the people you interviewed?"

Alex thought for a moment. "You could put them into two categories: people like Blake who have a background selling services, and people like Angie who have sold tangible products."

With his eyes scanning the horizon, Ted gave Alex the benefit of his experience. "I think you need to avoid Blake like the plague and hire a team full of Angies."

Alex was surprised at Ted's conviction. "How can you be so sure? Blake went to Cornell, his father knows a number of the CEOs in town, and he works at one of the top agencies in the country."

"In my experience, people like Blake, who are used to working in a service business, are good at consultative selling. They ask a lot of open-ended questions and probe for a client's needs. The clients reveal their innermost fears and then expect people like Blake to custom-tailor a solution. Blake will try to convince you to tailor the Five-Step Logo Design Process to meet the unique needs of each client."

"So why are you so sure Angie will work out?"

"From what you've told me about Angie, she will be fantastic. You have one process and you have packaged it to look like a product with five steps that don't change from one client to the next. Product salespeople are used to doing the mental gymnastics required to position their product to meet the needs of their prospect. A product salesperson doesn't have the luxury of changing their company's product every time they hear a need from a customer. They need to position the product they're stuck with to meet the customer's needs. That's exactly the kind of person you want selling the Five-Step Logo Design Process."

Alex took this in slowly. They sped along the water as the wind picked up.

TED'S TIP #9

Hire people who are good at selling products, not services. These people will be better able to figure out how your product can meet a client's needs rather than agreeing to customize your offering to fit what the client wants.

"That sounds counterintuitive to being a service provider."

Ted, not deterred by the wind speed and the increasing angle of the Laser, yelled back, "It is! Again, most service companies are not sellable other than for a long, risky, and painful earn-out. They depend on their owners to be the rainmakers. When the owner goes, there is no more business, and acquiring companies understand that. You need to stop doing the selling yourself and hand the reins to a team of people like Angie."

They sped toward the outer bay, where the waves were picking up. After a long silence, Ted upped the ante in their work together. "Alex, the next step in the process is going to take enormous courage on your behalf. Are you ready?"

"It can't take any more courage than sailing with you," Alex said, half joking.

"It's time you tell your existing clients that you will no longer be able to support their advertising needs because you are specializing in logo design."

Alex immediately calculated the implication of Ted's direction.

"Can I keep doing other work for MNY Bank?"

Ted was emphatic. "Absolutely not."

Alex reminded Ted of the financial impact of what he was suggesting, but Ted stood his ground.

"Alex, you can't be half pregnant. If you keep doing other work that falls outside of your logo design process, you'll send mixed messages to all of your stakeholders."

"Ted, MNY Bank accounted for 40 percent of our revenue last year."

"I know, and your business is unsellable as a result. If you keep offering custom services, you'll need to replace your senior designer and your copywriter and you'll telegraph to the market that you're not committed to your logo design process. MNY refuses to deal with anyone but you, so if you did sell, you'd be locked in for years. If a client is given the choice, they would always rather have a custom-tailored solution just for them. So if you run a custom service business in parallel to your logo design business, you won't be giving the Five-Step Logo Design Process a chance to thrive."

"I'll need to think about that," Alex said.

"I warned you that you would need courage to take this step."

Out of the blue, Ted gestured for Alex to look down at the tiller in Ted's hands.

"I'm asking you to make a 180-degree turn in the way you think about your business. It's a little bit like a jibe." With that, Ted pulled the tiller hard toward him. The boat careened downwind and keeled over at what seemed to Alex like an impossible angle. The boom followed the boat's turn and swung violently from one side of the boat to the other. Ted pushed Alex over to the other side of the boat while he pulled in the sail and positioned himself next to Alex. The wind filled the sail with a *thwack*. Ted hiked out so that his feet were on the gunnels, and the boat started speeding for shore.

"To jibe properly, you need to pull the tiller all the way to one side. There's a moment when you feel a little out of control just before the sail flips sides and starts catching wind on the other side of the turn. You can't half commit. If you don't pull the tiller all the way toward you, you'll never turn the boat and you'll end up in the water. I'm asking you to jibe the Stapleton Agency."

7   Growing Pains

Angie's first week at the Stapleton Agency was productive. Alex asked her to divide the prospect list into four territories based on quadrants of the city. Angie recommended one of her former colleagues from her time at the yellow pages directory to join her as the second sales rep. Based on her recommendation, Alex met with Seamus O'Reilly.

Seamus was also in the top ten among sales reps at Angie's former company. The two had worked together and enjoyed the friendly competition of jostling for the top spot each month. In Seamus, Alex saw a lot of the same attributes he valued in Angie. He hired Seamus without hesitation.

Two weeks later, Seamus started at the Stapleton Agency. His first project was to erect a whiteboard in the middle of the office that detailed both sales reps' weekly sales statistics. Each day, they updated their number of appointments confirmed for the week and the number of logos sold. They each had a goal of one logo per week.

By the fourth week of selling, Angie was consistently setting up ten appointments per week. Seamus was up to eight per week. Finally, on the last Friday of the month, Angie sold her first logo. She raced into Alex's office with the signed contract. They both celebrated by ringing the bell Angie and Seamus had set up outside Alex's office. The entire agency heard the commotion and got up from their desks to join the celebration.

Alex beamed all the way home that night. Not only had he built a process others could deliver, but someone else other than him could sell it. It occurred to him as he pulled into his garage that he didn't even know the name of the company Angie had sold her first logo to. He reveled in the feeling of building something larger than himself.

———◆———

Alex agreed to meet with John Stevens at his office to discuss the Spanish version of MNY's new brochure. He rarely wore a suit, but for some reason decided to for this occasion.

The two exchanged pleasantries and John launched into a description of the changes he required for his brochure to ensure its suitability for the Hispanic market. Alex listened carefully. By the time he issued his last directive, John was collecting his things, signaling he was finished with him. Alex knew that it was now or never.

"John, it's been a pleasure working with you over the last few years. In fact, we've worked on a lot of different projects together. The logo we designed for the wealth management division last year stands out for me. Do you remember that project?"

"Of course, you guys did a great job. Listen Alex, I've got another meeting, so—"

"This will only take a second, John. The logo we did for your wealth management division was not unusual for us. In fact, we have had great success designing logos for a lot of clients. So much so that we have decided to specialize in creating logos."

"That's great, Alex. When can I see the first draft of the Spanish version of the brochure?"

"John, we'll get you the first version of the brochure next Monday, but this will be the last brochure we create for you. The trade-off for specializing in logo design is that we won't be able to accept other types of projects going forward."

"But Alex, MNY Bank gives you tens of thousands of dollars of work every month. I'm not sure you're in a position to dictate to us."

"I understand, John, and I appreciate the support you have given us, but that's the decision we've made and I hope we can continue to work together when you have new products to launch that need a logo."

"I have to say I'm disappointed. I mean, I applaud your focus, but I thought we were a special client."

"You are a special client, which is why I wanted to tell you in person."

Alex felt good about his decision. He had stood his ground and left John's office walking tall for the first time.

———◆———

Harry Stumberger had been Alex's accountant since he started the Stapleton Agency. Each quarter, Harry spent two days at the office, working with Alex's office manager, Olga, to ensure that collections were on track and that taxes were being paid on time. Harry would review the invoices Olga had produced and the expenses they had incurred, after which he would issue a profit-and-loss statement that detailed the agency's affairs for the previous three months.

Harry was scheduled to meet Alex at 10:00 a.m., and as usual, he arrived early. He stumbled into Alex's office fighting with his umbrella. Alex was huddling with Angie and Seamus reviewing the latest numbers on the whiteboard and called out to Harry as he arrived.

"Hey, come on in, Harry. Make yourself at home. I'll be in my office shortly."

Harry settled in by removing a pad of paper, a pencil, and a sharpener from his briefcase. He also extracted a laptop computer and a large blue file.

Five minutes later, Alex entered the office.

"Thanks for coming. How are we doing this quarter?"

Harry hesitated and then decided to tell it to Alex straight.

"Not well. You're on target to lose $12,000 this month and, unless things turn around, another $9,000 next month."

"How's that possible, Harry? We've been selling logos like crazy and we have a ton of cash in the bank."

"Your cash position is the one bright spot, but selling those logos is killing your business."

"I'm confused."

"For each logo you sell, you bill $10,000 up front, which is great for your cash flow. Unfortunately, according to generally accepted accounting principles, or GAAP, I need to apply that revenue in three equal installments starting with the month you sell it and ending three months later. That means I can only recognize $3,333.33 of the $10,000 you bill for a logo project this month. You've gone from recognizing the revenue from projects in the month you win them to recognizing revenue across three months. It is having the effect of cutting your monthly revenue by two-thirds on paper."

"So we're going to lose money this month?"

"Yes, and next month too unless you start accepting other projects again. And if this keeps up, you can forget about declaring a bonus this year. You'll be lucky to break even by the end of the year."

Alex listened to Harry and cursed Ted in his mind. He knew he should have accepted the USW project.

Alex flicked the wipers on high speed and just made out the entrance into Ted's underground parking garage through the rain. It was Tuesday and the combination of the rain and his meeting with Harry had dampened his mood.

The effervescent Cindy took his coat and provided a bright spot in Alex's morning. Ted was finishing up on the phone and waved him in. Alex took his normal spot on the big white leather chairs in front of the coffee table in Ted's office. Ted came over, greeted Alex, and asked for his regular update.

"Give me the numbers."

"Both Angie and Seamus are consistently getting eight to ten appointments per week. Angie closed five logos last month and Seamus closed four, so they are both tracking well against their goal of one logo per week each."

"That's great news, Alex. You must be thrilled."

"Yes and no. I met with Harry last week and he gave me some disturbing news."

"And what did Harry have to say?"

"Harry said I should have accepted the USW contract."

"Of course he did, Alex. Harry is paid to count the numbers. He does not have the context for what we are doing. He has no way of distinguishing the good, scalable revenue you get from selling logos from the bad, one-off revenue you get from projects. To Harry, it's all just revenue. Since your Five-Step Logo Design Process takes three months to deliver, he's legally obliged to account for that revenue on your profit-and-loss statement across three months. As you move from ad hoc project work to a single productized service, there will be a point where, on paper, you're in trouble. Let me ask you: How does your bank account look?"

"We have a lot of cash because we billed for all of the logos we sold up front. I'm surprised Mary hasn't called to invite me to lunch."

"While you're in the midst of making this change, you will show a loss on paper, and that's okay as long as your cash flow remains strong and you keep selling logos. In three months, you'll start entering months with revenue on the books from logos you sold this month. You will be starting each month with a base of revenue and adding to it with each logo sold. You need to sacrifice for the next three months until your paper statements catch up with the progress you're making."

"But my fiscal year closes in two months and I was planning to declare a bonus this year to pay off my mortgage. There won't be much profit for me to take out of the company."

"That's true, Alex. You'll probably need to trim your bonus this year. But think of this as very mild short-term pain for a very big gain down the road. If we can get someone to buy your business, you will be able to pay off ten mortgages. It's worth taking a small hit this year."

TED'S TIP #10

Ignore your profit-and-loss statement in the year you make the switch to a standardized offering even if it means you and your employees will have to forgo a bonus that year. As long as your cash flow remains consistent and strong, you'll be back in the black in no time.

"How am I supposed to sell a company without any profit?"

"Alex, creating a sellable business takes time. You're going to have to stick with me for the long haul."

"How long a haul are we talking?"

"I need you to give me two more years."

"Two years is a long time, Ted."

"Yes, but you've been running the Stapleton Agency for eight years. Wouldn't it be worth investing another two to finally get rewarded for all of your hard work? Besides, if you sold the business tomorrow—and I'm skeptical we could even find a buyer—they would only agree to buy your company if you signed on for a five-year earn-out. I'm really asking you for a two-year commitment as opposed to five. I'm actually going to save you three years."

"When you put it like that, I guess I can't refuse. I was getting excited about the prospect of selling and spending some more time with Pam and the kids. You know, Jenny will be entering high school this year, and Max is right behind her. I only have a few more years before they're off to college."

"I understand, Alex. The next two years will be hard work but they will also be much more enjoyable. Your cash flow will be strong. You will no longer be the 'go-to guy' for every client, which will reduce the number of client headaches you have. You'll probably be able to take some vacation time with the family. I think you'll find the next two years to be a lot more fun than the last two, and you will be able to have confidence in the fact that you're building something sellable."

TED'S TIP #11

You need at least two years of financial statements reflecting your use of the standardized offering model before you sell your company.

Pam Stapleton had been married to Alex for fourteen years. She'd encouraged Alex to start the Stapleton Agency and had been his greatest cheerleader over the years. But that was before the orthodontist bills and the mortgage. Now Pam had grown used to the bonus checks Alex brought home.

Alex knew he would need to break the news to her gently.

"Honey, I need to talk to you about the work I've been doing with Ted Gordon."

"Great, I've been meaning to ask you about your Tuesday sessions."

"We've made a lot of progress, but we're at a critical stage now and it's going to have an impact for us personally this year."

"What exactly are you talking about?" Pam said, hesitating.

"We're making some changes so that my business will be sellable in the long term. But in the short term, I'll make less money on paper. That means I won't be able to declare a bonus."

"But Alex, you promised we'd pay off the mortgage this year, and we told the kids we'd take them to Hawaii for spring break. We don't have the money for that trip just lying around."

"I know, and we can still go on vacation, but we'll just have to pick somewhere less expensive. We need to make some sacrifices this year, but if we do this right, I'll be able to sell my business and then we can take a lot more family vacations down the road."

Alex hugged his wife and promised himself he would make it up to her.

———◆———

Over the next few months, life at the Stapleton Agency found a steady rhythm. Angie and Seamus continued to sell roughly one logo each per week. Rhina enjoyed having a system to follow, and Chris was getting efficient at creating logos. The clients of the Stapleton Agency were for the most part satisfied with the results. Olga continued to march off to the bank every Friday afternoon with more checks to deposit. Things were going well enough for Alex to take a day away from the office to do some thinking.

———◆———

Alex inhaled the salt in the cool air as he stepped out of the car. Waves were breaking on shore as he walked along a path leading to the ocean. The trail cut through a tall sand dune that rose up more than sixty feet high on both sides. As the path turned south, the beach house came into view. It sat on its own with the next closest house at least five hundred feet down the beach. The entire structure was enclosed by windows, which reflected the sun as it rose in the east. The November morning meant that the beach was deserted. Alex imagined the hive of activity that must take place on a warm August afternoon.

It was off-season and none of Ted's family were using the beach house, so he had offered it to Alex for his planning session. Alex surveyed his home for the next twenty-four hours. He started in what appeared to be the family room. It was large with modern furniture positioned to take in the sunrise.

He opened a large set of double doors to discover what he assumed was the master bedroom, removed his shoes, and lay on the king-sized bed, imagining waking up to the sun rising over the horizon. A small teak table on the patio off the master bedroom separated two steamer chairs. In addition to the expansive master quarters, there was a doorway leading to a bathroom with a two-headed steamer shower and heated slate floors.

Off the kitchen there was a set of double doors, which opened onto a deck that stretched out for thirty feet and ran the circumference of the house. The hot tub crafted into the cedar was big enough for twelve people. He sized up the stainless steel Weber and determined that it had the perfect cooking surface for the ten-ounce filet resting in the fridge. This was going to be a good day.

Ted had agreed to lend Alex his beach house on the condition that Alex use some of the time to answer a simple question. Ted had written the question on a piece of paper and sealed it inside a small envelope, which he instructed Alex to open only after he got to the beach house. Intrigued, Alex opened the envelope. Inside was a single recipe card with a handwritten question scribbled on one side:

It was a question he had thought about a lot over the past eight years.

Alex thought about it from a variety of angles. First he asked himself what the business would be worth to someone else. With his year-end approaching next month, Harry had given him a preliminary snapshot of how he would likely end the year financially:

> Revenue: $1,400,000
> Expenses: $1,313,000
> Pretax Profit: $87,000

Alex understood that small service businesses like his typically sell for roughly three to four times pretax profit, which meant his business was worth less than $500,000. It wasn't enough.

Then he came at Ted's question from a different angle: What was the business worth to him? How much money did he need to feel free? The second number was a lot bigger. Given the wide gap between the two numbers, Alex decided to move on to the rest of his planning agenda but resolved to have Ted's question answered before he left the beach house.

He spent the rest of the morning planning the year ahead. He thought about the financial performance he would need to attract a buyer and knew that he had to significantly increase both his top and bottom line.

Angie and Seamus were reliably selling one logo each per week. They charged $10,000 per logo, so they would likely sell a little less than $1 million worth of logos. He scribbled numbers on a pad and played with various scenarios. He had confidence that he could find more salespeople, but he also wanted to balance what

Rhina and Chris could deliver. The Five-Step Logo Design Process was somewhat new, yet he definitely wanted to grow. He settled on a goal of $2.5 million in annual revenue and made a note that he would need to hire three more salespeople, as well as a new account director and designer to help Rhina and Chris manage the load.

Next, he turned his attention to his expenses. A pretax profit of 15 percent, or $375,000, was a reasonable goal given that he didn't have any hard costs associated with the business of creating logos. He went through his expenses line by line, looking for costs to cut to make his profit margin goal achievable. He vowed to drop his subscription to *Advertising Age* given that he no longer offered advertising. There was no need for freelance copywriters, and he didn't need to attend the American Association of Advertising Agencies' annual media conference in San Diego this year, since he no longer bought media for his clients. He was pleasantly surprised at the costs he could cut out of the company given his focus on logos. The 15 percent margin number seemed reasonable even with three extra salespeople and help for Rhina and Chris.

The morning had been a success, and Alex rewarded himself by tucking into the sandwich he had brought with him from the city. After lunch, he walked down to the beach. As he made his way along the shore, his mind wandered back to Ted's question: How much was eight years' work worth to him? How much was realistic? The questions kept coming, and Alex was no closer to an answer for Ted.

The rest of the afternoon was spent back at the beach house thinking through the changes he would need to make to support revenue of $2.5 million.

———•———

The Weber's automatic starter responded after just one depression of the knob. Alex put the grill on high and let it warm up for five minutes. He opened the bottle of Beringer he had bought and poured a glass but did not drink, opting instead to let the wine open up and embrace the sea air. With the grill at 400 degrees, Alex seared both sides of the meat and cooked it for five minutes. Dinner was ready.

He sliced a thin layer of steak and inspected the color—a perfect shade of pink. It tasted as good as it looked, and he washed his first piece down with a hearty mouthful of wine. He closed his eyes and savored the explosion of taste as the two flavors met.

Eating alone, Alex smiled and reflected on the progress he had made so far in working with Ted. Groveling for work from MNY Bank had been replaced by a steady stream of new customers; personally juggling the management of all of the clients had been replaced by Rhina following the instruction manual; and late-night calls to Mary Pradham had been replaced by figuring out how to invest his extra cash. His mind again turned to Ted's question. He poured himself another glass of California's finest. Perhaps encouraged by the wine, he decided to suspend the reality of what he thought his business was worth today and instead thought about how much money he would need to lead the life he dreamed of.

There were the requisite things he wanted, but overall he was surprised by how modest his material needs were. He liked his car. His house would need to be paid off. A beach house would be nice but not necessary. Maybe some travel with Pam and the kids. In all, his lifestyle needs were not that demanding. What he really craved was freedom. He had spent his working life at the beck and call of clients and was tired of having others tell him what to do. He wanted to feel free of needing to work. With the wine anesthetizing the reality of what his business was actually worth, Alex answered Ted's question.

He wanted to sell the Stapleton Agency for $5 million.

8   The Number

A lex felt a rush of satisfaction as he piloted the Range Rover back into the city. The big V-8 engine easily handled sixty miles an hour and hardly sounded like it was working at 2,000 RPM. It was still early, so after a quick stop for a Grande Bold, Alex headed directly to Ted's office to drop off the keys to the beach house.

Ted was getting off the phone and gestured to Alex to wait for him. The call ended and Alex handed Ted the keys.

"Thanks, Ted. Your place is fantastic."

"Glad you liked it, Alex. How did the planning go?"

"Good. I'm going to try to hit $2.5 million of revenue this year, and I'd like to improve our profit margin to 15 percent pretax."

"Those would be significant improvements over where you are today. Did you open the envelope?"

"I did."

"So, what's your number?"

Surprised by Ted's bluntness, Alex paused.

"First I came at it from the point of view of what I thought the business was worth. Then I looked at our goals, and then . . ." Ted listened patiently as Alex tried to explain his rationale. "I thought about the work I've put into the business to date, how much more work is left to get done over the next two years, and . . ."

Alex was nervous about revealing his number to Ted. He

looked up, hesitated a moment, and then said, "I want to get $5 million for my business."

Ted didn't flinch at hearing Alex's number. Instead, he offered a simple directive.

"I want you to do something for me. It may not be immediately clear why you need to do this today, but trust me, it will become clear down the road and you'll be glad you did. Take one of these recipe cards"—Ted handed him a card like the one he had used to write his question for Alex at the beach house—"and write down $5 million on this card. Then put it in this envelope and seal it."

"Sounds cryptic. Why do I need to write it down?"

"That will become clear later. Just write it down and put the envelope where you'll be able to find it in a couple of years."

Angie and Seamus continued to sell well through December. Despite the holidays, Angie sold six logos and Seamus sold five. Alex asked both Angie and Seamus to recommend salespeople they knew from their previous jobs. One of his friends had heard Seamus bragging about his new company and had expressed an interest in joining. Alex hired him after a short interview. Angie recommended a friend who was returning to the workforce after taking a couple of years away to start a family. Alex got the word out among his contacts and found the fifth sales rep he needed.

They helped their new colleagues get familiar with the selling system they had designed. In the meantime, Alex put the word out to his network that he was looking for a new account director. He interviewed six people, looking for someone with Rhina's attention to detail. He hired Belinda Carter away from a rental car agency where she had been thriving as a branch manager. Rhina and Belinda hired a coordinator to help with some of the details.

Alex contacted his alma mater where he had attended art school and let the professors know he was looking for designers who could freehand sketch and use the latest computer design programs. He asked Chris to meet with a few designers and collectively they picked out one who met their criteria.

The Stapleton Agency was growing: five salespeople, two account directors, two designers, one coordinator, and Olga managing the office and the books.

———◆———

The snow fell all night, making the morning drive to the office slower than usual. Alex parked in his usual spot, trudged through the slush to the building, and stepped inside. He shook off the snow and salt as best he could and made his way to his office. Angie was waiting for him leaning against his doorway. She stepped aside to let him in.

"Alex, can we talk for a few minutes?"

"Sure, Angie, let me just get my coat off . . ."

Angie didn't waste any time.

"I'm glad we brought in three new sales reps, but I'm getting stretched thin. They have a lot of questions, and I want to be helpful, but I'm getting to a point where my sales are starting to suffer. I know Seamus feels the same way."

Alex tried to ease Angie off the ledge. "Angie, I know you've been really helpful at bringing the new guys up to speed, and I appreciate all the extra time you've invested."

"That's great, but I think we're at a point now where you need to decide if you want me to sell or manage. I can't do both."

Alex agreed to get back to Angie with a resolution to her concerns next week.

———◆———

The last Tuesday of the month started as most other Tuesdays had in the past six months, with Alex offering Ted the week's numbers.

"February has been a good month so far," Alex reported. "Angie closed four logos, Seamus is at five for the month, and the new sales reps each sold their first logos."

"Alex, that's great news!"

"Yes, but our growth is starting to create some problems. Angie spends a lot of her time teaching the new sales reps our process. I know Rhina is feeling stretched as Belinda gets up to speed, and Chris has already said we need a third designer."

"Good," Ted said. "It's about time you built a management team."

"Sounds like something MNY would have."

"If you're going to sell your business, you need to demonstrate that it can run without you. You need to show a potential acquirer that you have a management team that can keep the business running when you're gone."

"Are you suggesting I bring in outside managers?"

"Not at all. Sounds like Angie, Rhina, and Chris are already your managers. You just need to make it official."

"I guess you're right. But isn't that going to be expensive?" Alex protested.

"Not necessarily," said Ted. "You need to align their compensation with your goals. You can do that with a small bonus and give them a chance to share in the growth of the Stapleton Agency."

"Are you talking about sharing equity with them?"

"Sharing equity can get messy. It's time-consuming, and why dilute your equity and complicate things when you don't have to?"

"So if not with equity, how else can I let them participate in our growth?"

"There are a lot of options," Ted explained. "You have to decide if you want to reward loyalty, in which case you might create a stay bonus tied to them being employed at some date in the future. Alternatively, you could create a performance bonus for achieving certain targets."

"What did you use in the businesses that you sold?"

"I used a long-term incentive plan designed to reward my managers' performance and their loyalty to the company."

"How did that work?" Alex asked.

"I gave managers targets and a corresponding bonus for achieving their personal targets. I paid them their bonus at the end of each year and put aside the exact same amount into a special pool of funds earmarked for them. Three years after launching the plan, and each year thereafter, they were allowed to withdraw one-third of the pool. That way, their pool grew in value each year corresponding with their personal achievements, but they could not access the extra money until three years after earning it. If they ever decided to leave, they would be walking away from three years' worth of bonuses sitting in the pool."

"I thought acquiring companies wanted to see that management had real equity . . ."

"In my experience, an acquiring company wants to see that there is a management layer in place and that the management team has some form of long-term incentive plan that will encourage them to stay after the business is purchased. One way to do that is with equity, but equity and stock options are complicated to set up and may cause you all sorts of headaches down the road. If I look at it from Angie, Rhina, and Chris's collective point of view, a long-term incentive plan like the one I used in my businesses has a lot of benefits over equity. In a small service business, equity is only worth anything if there is a market for the shares. Assuming the Stapleton Agency will never go public—and I think that is a safe bet—then you may decide not to sell, and then their shares are not worth

TED'S TIP #12

Build a management team and offer them a long-term incentive plan that rewards their personal performance and loyalty.

much. As an employee, I'd much rather have an understandable cash bonus plan than a few shares in a closely held small business."

As they wrapped up the meeting, Ted asked Alex to spend the next week considering how he wanted to structure the compensation of his management team.

Alex promoted Angie to vice president of sales, Rhina to vice president of client services, and Chris to vice president and creative director. His new management team was thrilled with their new titles. He gave them each a 7 percent pay raise and introduced a long-term incentive plan similar in design to the one Ted had described at their last meeting. Alex explained to his new management team that they were still a small business, they would each need to continue to do their jobs as before, and their promotion was designed to recognize them for the extra management tasks they were being asked to take on.

Alex left the office on Friday with a sense of satisfaction. He'd created and focused on a standard process that others could deliver, built a sales engine that produced excess cash, and established a management team with a long-term incentive plan.

He was close to having a sellable business.

9   Gaining Momentum

The next few months at the Stapleton Agency progressed according to Alex's plan. The new salespeople thrived under Angie's leadership. Rhina's attention to detail made her an excellent manager. Chris hired a third designer and continued to improve the efficiency of the Five-Step Logo Design Process. According to Harry, the financial results for the first six months of the year were equally impressive:

> Revenue: $1,280,000
> Expenses: $995,000
> Pretax Profit: $285,000

At the halfway point of the year, Alex was tracking to exceed both his revenue targets and his profit margin goal.

Mary Pradham asked to meet Alex over lunch, which was strange. He'd not heard from Mary for six months; his accounts were in good standing; and he usually met her at her office at the downtown branch of MNY Bank, not over lunch at one of the city's best restaurants.

The waiter arrived and Mary ordered sparkling water for the table. They worked through a painful few minutes of small talk.

Mary had never asked Alex about his personal life, so she didn't have much of a foundation to work from. She resorted to weather and sports. She was stretching, and it showed.

After their lunch arrived and the waiter left, Alex brought the conversation back to business.

"It's been a while since we spoke last. Why did you want to have lunch?"

"I like to meet with all of my clients face-to-face a few times a year," Mary exaggerated. "It's been a while since I've seen you, and judging by your account activity, you guys have been busy."

Alex decided to put Mary out of her misery early and took her question as a springboard to describe their new focus on logos, charging up front, the sales engine, and the building of his team.

"That's great, Alex. I think I have some other clients who could benefit from your focus."

Lunch plates were cleared and coffee arrived. Mary got down to business.

"I think I can get you a better rate of return on the money you have on deposit with us."

Alex nodded and gestured for Mary to continue.

She looked around to see if anyone was in earshot, lowering her voice as she spoke.

"As of this morning, you have $230,000 in your account, and judging by the pattern of your deposits, you're not going to need that money in the foreseeable future. Have you ever thought about high-yield CDs?"

Alex listened politely as Mary droned on about FDIC insurance and interest rates.

After an exhaustive summary of the many features of MNY Bank's deposit products, Mary launched into her next pitch. "If you ever want to expand, we'd be there to support you."

"What exactly do you mean by 'support you'?" Alex asked, tiring of Mary's duplicity.

"We have very good rates on credit lines. You have a $150,000 line of credit now, but I'm sure I could get the credit group to up that to $300,000, maybe more . . ."

Alex couldn't believe his ears. In the space of six months, Mary had gone from hounding him like a loan shark to offering a credit line increase over lunch at one of the better restaurants in town. The irony was breathtaking. He thought about calling Mary on her change of tune, but instead just smiled, sat back, and relished being courted by MNY Bank.

———— • ————

The second half of the year progressed well. Angie's team was consistently selling one logo per week. Rhina had taken the instruction manual for the Five-Step Logo Design Process to an entirely new level of detail that Alex was convinced would rival a lunar landing briefing. Chris was busy and enjoyed mentoring his growing team of young designers. With five weeks left to go, Harry projected the year would end as follows:

Revenue: $2,715,000
Expenses: $2,225,000
Pretax Profit: $490,000

Alex was looking forward to spending a day planning his next year.

———— • ————

It rained all day at the beach house. Alex marveled at the power of the ocean and the beauty of watching the storm from Ted's retreat. Given the weather, he spent an uninterrupted day planning.

The past year had been full of milestones: Angie and her team had more than doubled sales. Chris's designers had created more than 250 logos, and judging by the number of clients who were coming back to see Rhina for new product and division launches, she had cultivated a happy group of repeat customers.

Alex had built a foundation on which he could grow. He decided to set his annual target at $5 million in revenue with a 20 percent pretax profit margin. That night, he drafted an e-mail to update Ted on his progress:

> Ted:
> Thanks for letting me use your beach house for my annual planning again this year. I'm going to shoot for $5,000,000 in revenue and $1,000,000 in pretax profit! I'll give you the details when I see you on Tuesday.
> Alex

Alex started their Tuesday meeting with a quick update of the numbers. Ted listened and smiled at Alex's progress. He got up from his chair and walked over to the window, then turned to face Alex.

"When we first started our work together, the Stapleton Agency was a miserable business to own. Your team was being asked to do work they were not qualified to do; you were doing all of the sales and account management; your cash flow was tight; and you hadn't had a vacation in a while."

Alex cast his mind back to life eighteen months ago. "Yes, it seems like a long time ago. I'm having a lot more fun now."

"I thought you might be, which is why I want to revisit your decision to sell your company. If this year goes as planned, you're on track to generate $1 million in pretax profit. Your business is not as stressful as it used to be. You're not in a capital-intensive business, and with your positive cash flow cycle, you could probably declare a big bonus this year and keep growing the company as you have been doing."

Alex sat silently absorbing Ted comments. He'd been on a one-track journey to sell the business for more than a year and hadn't indulged himself in thoughts of a different strategy.

Ted asked Alex to join him at his desk so they could both look at his computer monitor. Ted had created a spreadsheet with two columns on it. The first column was labeled with the date one year from today. The second column was dated six years from today. Ted had plugged in some numbers in rows labeled *Revenue*, *EBITDA*, and *Multiple*.

"What's with the spreadsheet?"

"Alex, if you achieve a pretax bottom line of $1 million this year, you may be able to sell your business for $5 million, which was the goal you had when we met more than a year ago."

With this declaration, Ted pointed to a field on his spreadsheet labeled *Sale Proceeds* and the number $5,000,000 filled the cell. Alex couldn't help but crack a smile at the thought.

"However, you could choose to keep your business. You would need to shoulder all of the risk, and there would be tough patches. But if you kept the business for five more years and grew it at 20 percent per year—which is conservative given the pace you have been growing recently—your business could be worth $12 million or more."

Ted pointed to the spreadsheet. "Selling your business is a big decision. The process will be stressful and will take a toll on you and your family. Once you sell, there is no going back. I'd like you to spend the week thinking about whether you've made the right decision. When you come back next week, if you still want to sell your company, we'll get started with the final steps in the process."

———— ·•· ————

Alex needed to think and had to be away from the office. He found a Starbucks near Ted's office, ordered a Grande Bold, and sat in a quiet corner. He opened his notebook to an empty page and did what his mother had always taught him to do when he faced a big decision: He drew a line vertically down the center of the page and wrote the *Pros* on the left and *Cons* on the right. He started to scribble.

Selling Now

PROS   CONS

Time to Travel with Pam   Give up the possibility
                                  of a larger payout

Time with Jenny and Max

Pay off mortgage

Financial freedom

Less stress

Alex looked at the list and kept recalling the numbers Ted had calculated in their meeting. Five million dollars symbolized financial freedom. A financial planner had once told him that he could live on 4 percent of his investments in perpetuity. That meant that, after he paid tax on the sale of his business, he'd still have enough to draw a six-figure income each year from his nest egg for the rest of his life and never have to touch the principal. Jenny and Max would not be able to attend private school, but they'd have their dad around, and Pam would be happy that the bank would take the guarantee off their home and their financial affairs would finally be secure.

Then Alex contemplated $12 million. With that much money, he'd have more than enough money to pay off his mortgage and travel. Then his imagination failed him. Alex could not think of any toys that were worth the risk. The marginal value of the extra $7 million was limited and the risks were considerable. If he kept the business another five years, the economy could turn, or a competitor could decide to specialize in logos. Angie could set up a competitive shop, he could be sued . . . Alex let his mind get carried away with doomsday scenarios.

He would rather have $5 million today than a chance for $12

million in five years. Perhaps that made him weak. Maybe Ted would think he was not a real businessman. It didn't matter—he'd made his decision to sell.

—————◆—————

Ted joined Alex on the chairs they had used every Tuesday morning for the last eighteen months.

"Ted, thanks for creating the spreadsheet and forcing me to rethink my motivations for selling."

"You're welcome. It's a big decision."

"It is, and I feel more confident than ever with my decision to sell my firm. At the end of the day, I'm a simple guy. I don't need a vacation home in Aspen or a private plane. I want to experience true financial freedom, and $5 million would be enough."

"I'm glad you thought it through again and I'm happy to help you through the process. I want you to prepare yourself for a tough road. These last few steps will likely take six to eight months and it will be a bit of a roller coaster."

"I'm ready, Ted."

"Good. I think we're at a point where we need to start interviewing an adviser to represent you."

"You mean like an agent? Are you sure I need one?"

"A good broker will get you competitive offers and hopefully ask a lot of the tough questions behind the scenes."

"What kind of broker do you recommend?"

"Brokers come in all shapes and sizes. The ideal is to find a broker for whom you will be a meaningful account. The term *business broker* is usually used for individuals who do smaller deals where the total value of the transaction is well under $5 million. You're really looking for a boutique mergers and acquisitions firm. The firm you select needs to be large enough to be respected by a potential buyer, yet small enough that your deal will be important to them. Ideally they will have also done some deals in your industry."

TED'S TIP #13

Find an adviser for whom you will be neither their largest nor their smallest client. Make sure they know your industry.

"Do you know anyone I could speak to?" Alex asked.

"I'd recommend you speak with Mark Travers. He's with Travers Capital Partners; Cindy can give you his number. Also speak with Peggy Moyles. Peggy is a partner with EMG Capital Partners."

The office of Travers Capital Partners was downtown. The receptionist looked bemused as Alex approached. She greeted him coolly and assured him that Mr. Travers would be down to greet him shortly. After ten minutes, a woman walked through a set of doors and introduced herself as Amanda, Mark Travers's assistant. She instructed Alex to follow her up a spiral staircase that connected the two floors of Travers Capital Partners.

Amanda ushered Alex into a boardroom looking out over the city. Alex counted twelve Aeron chairs situated around a large glass boardroom table. He felt a little self-conscious sitting at such an oversized table, so he situated himself on one end near the door. Amanda returned and produced a large bottle of Perrier. There was a tall glass with ice and three neatly cut limes on the edge of a silver serving plate. Alex passed the time looking at a muted flatscreen television with CNBC rolling through stock quotes as if the capital markets were some sort of spectator sport. Finally, Mark Travers appeared, offering a firm handshake and a toothy smile.

"So, Alex, how do you know Ted Gordon?"

"He's an old family friend. How did you meet Ted?"

"We represented the buyer of Ted's consulting business. He's a smart guy and a tough negotiator. Tell me a little bit about your agency."

"We're not really an agency anymore. We specialize in producing logos. We do a lot of logos for companies launching new divisions or new products."

"Interesting. We know a lot of the marketing agencies in town. Who's your creative director?"

"His name is Chris Sawchuk and I doubt you know him. We don't consider ourselves a marketing agency per se. Our Five-Step Logo Design Process is all we do. We've become very efficient at creating logos."

Mark started to wave his hands, which Alex took to mean he had received some sort of flash of brilliance from above. Alex stopped to let Mark say whatever had gotten him so animated.

"I know the perfect company to buy your business," Mark declared.

Alex was surprised to hear that Mark already had an idea of who would buy the Stapleton Agency after just a few minutes of discussion. Intrigued, he asked Mark to elaborate.

"Look, we do a lot of work for Multicom," Mark said.

Alex recognized Multicom as the largest agency holding company in the world, with more than $1 billion in annual revenue and operations around the world.

"The Stapleton Agency is just the kind of tuck-in acquisition Multicom would love," Mark continued. "I'd be happy to arrange a meeting with their North American business development executive."

"Sounds great, Mark. How do you guys work with your clients?"

Mark went on to explain that they charged 5 percent of the deal but typically worked with much larger companies. He said under normal circumstances he would not take on a firm as small as the Stapleton Agency, but since Ted had referred Alex and he already had a good relationship with Multicom, he'd represent Alex as a favor to Ted.

Alex left Travers Capital Partners with mixed feelings. On one hand, he thought Mark was successful and certainly well connected to Multicom. On the other hand, something didn't seem quite right. It all sounded a little too easy.

———◆———

Alex's next meeting was with Peggy Moyles at EMG Capital Partners. She greeted Alex and ushered him into her office. Peggy asked him to describe his business, and Alex proceeded to outline the work they had done to remake the Stapleton Agency into a company with a single offering.

"Alex, you've done something most business owners never do, which is to extract yourself from the epicenter of your operations. You have a predictable sales engine with a good pipeline of recurring revenue. Your positive cash flow will be attractive to buyers, your capital structure is simple, and the management team seems to be engaged for the long term. You've built an excellent business."

"Thanks, Peggy. I had an exploratory meeting yesterday with Mark Travers over at Travers Capital Partners and he thought we would be a good fit for Multicom. What are your thoughts on Multicom as a potential buyer?"

"They would not have been my first choice. Big agencies have a standard formula by which they buy companies, and it typically involves a three- to five-year earn-out. In addition, big agencies think all companies want to be like them. I don't think they would value or appreciate all the work you've done to specialize in a single process."

Alex was impressed with Peggy's appreciation of the work he had done to move away from the agency model. He pressed her for some names of possible buyers.

"I'd like to have the opportunity to think about it some more," said Peggy, "but off the top of my head, I could see one of the technology firms with a big investment in color printing hardware, or maybe a large printing company might be interested. You could act as a Trojan horse for a company that wants the printing contracts of the companies you create logos for."

Alex liked the way Peggy was thinking.

She went on to describe how her firm worked. They charged 5 percent of the deal but also wanted a retainer of $7,000 per month over the next six months. Alex asked Peggy if she would waive the retainer and her response was crisp.

"We need to charge a retainer to ensure that you're serious about selling your business. If we took on assignments without a retainer, we'd spin our wheels generating offers for owners who were not serious about selling their firms."

Alex understood Peggy's position, but wondered why Mark Travers wasn't charging a retainer.

◆—◆—◆

Alex started their Tuesday meeting with a description of the meetings with Mark Travers and Peggy Moyles.

"So who are you going to go with?" Ted asked

"I'm not sure. I like that Mark knows the Multicom guys. He seemed to think it would be possible to get an offer from Multicom in the next few weeks."

"I understand, Alex, but if you want my advice, I'd avoid using Mark. It sounds like he wants to deliver a gift to Multicom in an effort to ingratiate his firm. Mark makes a lot of his money from representing buyers, and Multicom is a big client of his. It sounds like he would try to deliver you to Multicom without creating any competitive tension. Without that competition, you might be disappointed by Multicom's offer and you would have wasted a lot of time."

"I never considered that, but is there anything wrong with going with Mark to see if he can get a good offer from Multicom? Since he's not charging a retainer, I don't see what I have to lose."

"Once you engage an M&A firm, the chances others will find out you are interested in selling will go up. Mark will agree to keep things confidential, but the more people know of your intentions, the higher the chances are it will get back to your staff or customers."

Alex pondered Ted's warning for a moment and switched gears.

"Peggy wants a retainer."

"That's not necessarily a bad thing. She's going to act for you exclusively and she will still be motivated because most of her compensation will come from getting you a deal. She's a professional and needs some way of making sure you're serious. Plus, Peggy appreciates the fact that you're not just another marketing agency."

"You have a lot more experience with using M&A firms, so I'm inclined to choose Peggy based on what you're saying."

"I think she'll serve you well."

TED'S TIP #14

Avoid an adviser who offers to broker a discussion with a single client. You want to ensure there is competition for your business and avoid being used as a pawn for your adviser to curry favor with his or her best client.

10 A Blank Check for Growth

Once hired, Peggy asked Alex to provide a three-year business plan for the Stapleton Agency. She wanted Alex to include financial projections along with a description of the target market and the overall opportunity Alex envisioned for the business of creating logos. Peggy explained that Alex's plan would become the foundation for a lot of her work and it was important for the plan to be solid.

Alex had never planned more than one year in advance and found the process of writing a three-year plan daunting. One assumption led to the next, and by year three of the plan he felt like he was writing a work of fiction. In writing the financial projections, he anticipated a 20 percent top-line growth rate for the next three years. He kept his 20 percent profit margin goal steady. Once the plan was complete, Alex e-mailed it to Ted to get his input.

———◆———

Ted asked Alex to meet him at Starbucks across the street from his office.

"Good morning, Alex," Ted said, smiling. "What are you having?"

Ted turned to the barista and ordered a Grande Bold and a bottle of water. They found a quiet table in the corner and Alex began.

"What do you think of the plan?"

"It's a good start. Before we get into the plan, I want to talk coffee."

Alex was puzzled. "I noticed you ordered water. We didn't have to meet here for my benefit. You know we could have—"

"No. I wanted to meet here to talk about Starbucks. They've built an amazing business, don't you think?"

Alex didn't know where Ted was going with this but continued to play along. "They have stores on just about every street corner in America."

"And they're all pretty much the same. They even have their own language that you coffee drinkers have all learned fluently."

"What does this have to do with my plan?"

"Alex, I'm challenging you to sprinkle a little Starbucks in your plan."

"What do you mean?"

"When a company looks for an acquisition, it's usually because they want to grow. Often, they are not able to grow as fast as they want organically, so they acquire companies to bolster their top-line revenue. For you to get the highest valuation for the Stapleton Agency, you need to show how you can be an engine of growth for an acquirer."

"What does that have to do with Starbucks?" Alex asked.

"When you write your next draft, think about how aggressively Starbucks has grown. Imagine that you have a blank check to grow the Stapleton Agency as large and as fast as you possibly could given unlimited resources. You need to paint the picture for an acquirer of what is possible for the business of creating logos."

"But isn't that like lying?"

"Not at all. Your plan has to be possible but not necessarily achievable on your own. Peggy is going to approach companies that are a lot larger than you. They will have more money, more physical offices, more employees, more of everything. If you can plug the Stapleton Agency into a big company's resources, you will be able to grow much more quickly than you could on your own."

"How do I write the plan without knowing who the acquirer will be and exactly what resources they have?"

"The best way to do it at this point is to imagine you have a blank check and unlimited resources. There will be plenty of time for an acquiring company to scrutinize your plan and discount your projections based on what they think is reasonable. I want you to take off your conservative business owner hat and imagine what is possible. Could you start a satellite office in every major city in the country? Could you double your sales force? Could you make better use of the Internet to sell logos? Think like Starbucks."

Ted wished Alex luck and left. Alex ordered a refill and started scribbling notes.

Draft two of the plan was more fun to write. Alex suspended reality and imagined satellite sales offices of the Stapleton Agency in Houston, Chicago, Los Angeles, New York, and Atlanta. He planned a telephone operation with eight phone reps selling the Five-Step Logo Design Process to small businesses in rural America with no access to design resources. The new plan called for revenue of $12 million in three years. The more Alex wrote, the more

TED'S TIP #15

Think big. Write a three-year business plan that paints a picture of what is possible for your business. Remember, the company that acquires you will have more resources for you to accelerate your growth.

he believed the plan was actually possible if he found the right acquirer.

Alex e-mailed draft two of the plan to Ted. Ted's response came over e-mail a few hours later:

> Alex:
>
> I like the new plan. Lots of Starbucks—I think it will serve you well.
>
> I'd recommend you make one small change: Stop referring to this year's financials as a "Forecast." You need to communicate that you're confident in this year's projections. Instead, refer to your projections for this year as "Current Year." By the time we get to the offer stage, you will be three-quarters of the way through this year and you want an acquiring company basing their offer on $5 million in revenue and $1 million in profit, not last year's numbers. It's a subtle shift but it's important.
>
> Great job!
>
> Ted

Alex walked over to the whiteboard in the middle of the office. He saw that his salespeople were tracking well to plan. Each rep had at least six appointments set for the week and they were each on target to sell four logos for the month.

He walked back to his office and opened draft two of the plan on his desktop. He found the page that referred to his financial goals for this year and replaced the word "Forecast" with "Current Year."

Peggy Moyles was in her late forties. Salads for lunch and a daily appointment with a treadmill ensured that she looked five years younger. She had just come from a lunchtime Pilates class designed to help her posture, which on the occasion of her first working session with Alex was good. She offered Alex a firm handshake as he arrived at the offices of EMG Capital Partners.

She took Alex to a small boardroom where she arranged two copies of the plan Alex had e-mailed her, pencils, a calculator, and two bottles of water.

"Alex, the purpose of today's meeting is for me to understand your plan in enough detail that I can write a two-page teaser about your business and start work on the Book."

Alex needed a primer on the language of a deal. "What's a teaser?"

"A teaser is a one- or two-page description of your business, which announces that your company is for sale and paints the picture of the opportunity your business offers a potential buyer."

"But won't my employees and customers find out that the company is for sale?"

"No. We disguise the teaser so that your business is anonymous. If an acquiring company is interested, we'll send them a nondisclosure agreement. If they sign the NDA, then we'll send them a complete description of your business and your plan. We call that the Book."

"How many people will you send the teaser to?"

"Ideally, we should agree to a short list of around twenty companies. I've started a long list, and I'd like your help to narrow it down to just the companies with a compelling strategic reason to acquire the Stapleton Agency."

"I've heard about strategic buyers and financial buyers. I assume you're recommending we look for a strategic buyer."

"Strategic buyers will typically pay more because you're worth more to them than you would be to a financial buyer. A strategic buyer will model how you would perform as a business if they owned you and applied all of their resources to your business. A financial buyer is simply looking for a return on their investment and wouldn't bring much more than their checkbook to a deal. With few synergies to exploit, financial buyers will typically offer you a lower price to ensure they get a good return on their money."

"So which companies do you think would have a strategic reason to buy us?" Alex asked.

Peggy pulled out her long list of potential buyers and showed it to Alex.

"As you review it, consider the companies that have approached you for a partnership. Think about your suppliers and other companies you come into contact with. Your plan calls for more offices and more salespeople, so think about companies that already have a lot of salespeople or offices in other cities. Which companies have the most synergies to exploit?"

Peggy and Alex brainstormed companies and rated each one for their strategic fit. After two hours, Peggy narrowed the list to twenty-three companies with a compelling strategic reason to acquire the Stapleton Agency. Each company had enough cash to buy Alex's company and, as far as Peggy was aware, was open to the idea of an acquisition.

For the first time that spring, Alex opened the sunroof. It was the last Tuesday in March and the sun showed the first signs of warmth after a long winter.

Alex started their Tuesday get-together with a description of his meeting with Peggy. Ted waved him off.

"Before we talk about Peggy, give me this week's numbers."

Alex was caught off guard, as he had expected Ted to want to spend their Tuesday time on Peggy's work. Nevertheless, he thought back to the whiteboard and summarized their progress.

"We're on track. Angie's team sold eight logos last week, which makes twenty-seven for the month, and we still have three selling days left in the month. Rhina just hired another account director, so she now has five people on her team. Chris is interviewing another designer next week, and our old client Natural Foods has come back again for another logo. This time Ziggy is launching a line of organic chocolate milk."

"I thought tree huggers were all about healthy living," Ted said with a cheeky grin.

Having dispensed with the banter, Ted got serious. "Alex, your work with Peggy is going to eat up a lot of your time. As hard as it is going to be, you have to keep your eyes on the Stapleton Agency's performance. You have to make sure your current-year projections are achieved."

"I'll keep my eye on the ball," Alex said.

"There's one other thing I want you to think about. I noticed you used the word 'client' to describe Natural Foods."

"Yes. Ziggy's been a client of ours for a while."

"That's good, but I want you to replace the word 'client' with the word 'customer' when you talk about the companies that buy your process."

Alex couldn't believe Ted was nitpicking over a single word. "Why does that matter?"

"Service firms refer to their customers as clients and product businesses refer to them as customers. You've worked hard to transform the Stapleton Agency from a service business into a product business with a standard scalable and repeatable process. Using words like 'client' subtly communicates to a potential buyer that you still think of yourself as a service business."

"It's just a word. Surely that can't matter to a potential buyer," Alex said.

"At this point in the process, appearances matter a lot. An acquiring company will be trying to put you in a box in their mind. They have a box for product companies and a corresponding process for acquiring them. They have a different box in their mind for acquiring service businesses, and you don't want to land in that box."

"Why not?"

"Because their service business box has a formula for acquiring a business that uses a three- to five-year earn-out with only a small amount of cash up front. If you land in their service business box, you'll get an offer with most of your money at risk and tied to an earn-out. You take all of the risk and they get most of the reward. You're going to have to agree to leave some of your money in an earn-out, but our goal is to get you as much cash up front as you can. That means doing whatever you can to communicate the fact that the Stapleton Agency is not a plain old service business."

TED'S TIP #16

If you want to be a sellable, product-oriented business, you need to use the language of one. Change words like "clients" to "customers" and "firm" to "business." Rid your Web site and customer-facing communications of any references that reveal you used to be a generic service business.

"So I need to start referring to clients as customers."

"Yes. And think about the other words you use that are the typical lingo of a service business. I'd stop calling the Stapleton Agency a 'firm' and start referring to it as a 'business' instead. Replace the word 'engagement' with the word 'contract.' You want to do whatever you can to communicate to a buyer that you're a real business, not just a flighty collection of temperamental professional service providers."

11   Telling Management

Ît was well after 5:00 p.m. by the time Alex returned from his meeting with Peggy, and the Stapleton Agency was still a hive of activity. Alex felt like an unfaithful spouse returning from an encounter with a lover as he mingled with his staff.

"Hey, Angie, how was your day?"

"The team's doing well. We've closed two deals and have scheduled nine new appointments this afternoon. The guys are staying late because I promised them drinks were on me if they could schedule twenty appointments in a single afternoon."

Smiling at how much Angie enjoyed motivating her flock, Alex sauntered over to Rhina's office, expecting her to be gone for the day. Rhina was still in the office and meeting with one of her account directors on the Natural Foods chocolate milk assignment.

Rhina saw Alex approaching and waved him over. "We found out today that if Natural Foods were a famous Hollywood star, they would be Sarah Jessica Parker," she said with a smile.

"How is my friend Ziggy doing?" Alex asked.

"She's great and says hi."

Alex continued his tour and saw Chris at his desk proofing one of the logos that was about to go to stage five of the process. This surprised Alex less, because Chris had been working late for the past four days.

"Don't sleep here tonight," Alex said jokingly.

"I won't. We're just about finished for the day," Chris said optimistically.

Alex felt a pang of guilt as he walked back to his office. His staff was working well after 5:00 p.m. while he had spent the day contemplating the sale of his business. Alex knew he would be the only one to gain financially from the sale of the Stapleton Agency, and somehow that didn't seem right.

It was unusually cold for the first week in April and Alex stuffed his hands into the pockets of his raincoat as he jogged from his car to the offices of EMG Capital Partners. He was meeting with Peggy at her office to discuss the teaser distribution.

She began with a summary of their progress to date. All twenty-three companies short-listed had been contacted. Seven companies had declined, saying they were working on other deals, while four companies had requested the Book and agreed to sign the NDA. Peggy was waiting to hear back from the remaining twelve companies.

"Great progress," Alex said.

"Yes, we're happy with the reaction to the teaser so far. It's still in the early days, but so far so good."

"What's the next step in the process once the Book has been distributed?"

"We need to schedule management presentations with the interested parties."

"I'll need to meet with these people in person?"

"Yes."

Peggy sat quietly, considering whether it was the right time to raise a delicate issue. Her rapport with Alex had been good so far, so she decided to proceed.

"Alex, as part of the management presentations, we'll need to involve your management team. It's important for a potential buyer to see the next layer of management who will be responsible for the business if and when you leave."

"If I tell them I'm thinking of selling, I have no idea how they'll react. I mean, they helped me to build our business. They put their heart and soul into our success. There's no telling how they'll react when I tell them I'm selling out."

"You'll need to tell them sooner or later. And I'd recommend sooner. Even if I can convince a prospective buyer to meet with you on your own for the management presentation, eventually they will want to meet your team. Plus, as more people get the Book, despite the NDA, the higher the odds are that one of your team will find out. I'm sure you'd rather tell them directly than have them find out some other way."

Alex left Peggy's office wondering how to tell Angie, Rhina, and Chris that the guy they had placed their faith in and worked so hard for was about to sell out to the highest possible bidder.

———— • ————

Ted was immersed in something at his desk as Alex arrived. Alex shared the week's sales numbers and gave an update on his progress with Peggy.

Sensing there was something else on Alex's mind, Ted asked, "Alex, you seem a little introspective today. What are you thinking about?"

"Peggy thinks we're going to have three or four companies interested in making an offer, and the next stage in the process involves management presentations."

"That's great news."

"I guess so, but Peggy thinks each of the bidders will need to meet with Angie, Rhina, and Chris, so I'll have to tell them I'm thinking of selling the business."

"That's a delicate conversation. What are your biggest concerns?"

"I feel guilty. I think they're going to look at me and resent the fact that I'm cashing in."

"Alex, I understand the way you're feeling. I felt the same way when I sold my first business."

"And how did your employees take it?"

"At first they were a little surprised, but after they had time to process the news, they started to warm to the idea."

"They actually liked the idea?"

"Yes. Working for a small business can have advantages, but the possibilities for career advancement are limited. They look at the highest rung of the ladder every time you walk into the office and know that as long as you own the business, they can only ascend so high."

"I get that they might see career opportunities, but it's hard to integrate two companies, and there are always redundancies . . ."

"Merging two companies can be a challenge. However, there are also a lot of opportunities that emerge when a big company swallows a small one. Ambitious people want to paint on a bigger canvas. Big companies have big budgets and important projects, and operate on a level of professionalism that your best people will enjoy. If they play it right, Angie, Rhina, and Chris could benefit from some career mobility if you are acquired."

"They may see opportunities, but aren't they going to be jealous that I walk away with a check and all they get is a new boss?"

"Alex, you've worked hard to build the Stapleton Agency. You took all of the risk, and, for better or worse, capitalism rewards risk taking. It was you who trudged up to MNY Bank every other day groveling for work. You were the one who lost sleep every time Mary Pradham called. It was your home the bank would have taken had you defaulted on your operating line."

"But I'd still like to find a way to let them benefit financially if we are acquired."

"Fair enough. Keep in mind they will each benefit personally if a strategic buyer acquires you, because the acquirer will come with strategic assets—like offices in other cities and investment dollars—that will make it easier for Angie, Rhina, and Chris to reach their personal objectives and corresponding bonuses. They also have a long-term incentive plan that will pay out at higher levels corresponding with their higher bonuses."

"Maybe I should throw in some stock options as well to sweeten the deal for my team. They've been with me for a while."

"Your intentions are admirable but misguided. Stock options will further complicate the process of selling your business. You'll have to draft a shareholders' agreement. Minority shareholders have rights. You will be morally, and to some extent legally, required to keep Angie, Rhina, and Chris in the loop as you review offers. Selling your business is hard enough. You don't need three other opinions at the table. My advice would be to keep it clean and give your management team a simple, one-time cash bonus if you successfully sell your business as a thank-you for helping you with the management meetings and their dedication to the business. That way you're giving them a cash incentive to participate in the

TED'S TIP #17

Don't issue stock options to retain key employees after an acquisition. Instead, use a simple stay bonus that offers the members of your management team a cash reward if you sell your company. Pay the reward in two or more installments only to those who stay so that you ensure your key staff stays on through the transition.

management meetings and sharing in your rewards. But I wouldn't get carried away. They're already benefiting from the chance of career advancement and a higher probability of achieving their personal bonus targets and corresponding long-term incentive plan."

Alex left Ted's office feeling better about the prospects of telling his management team.

A meeting with Angie, Rhina, and Chris was arranged for the last Friday in April. Alex was not one for early morning meetings, so his leadership team was already buzzing about the possible reasons for the meeting.

He greeted his team and was surprised at how nervous he felt. Alex had made important presentations to larger audiences full of people he didn't know. He was about to present to just three people he'd known and worked with for more than a year, yet he was noticeably nervous.

"Thanks for coming in early for this session. I wanted to start early to ensure we don't get interrupted by the rest of the team. I've been spending a lot of time out of the office over the last few months to plan the next stage of our growth as a company. I think you guys have proven that we have a scalable model for creating logos. We've done well here in town and I think we can do even more if we start to expand geographically."

The team sat up in their seats, proud to be working for a successful, growing company and excited about the prospect of new locations and growing the business.

"It's become clear to me that for us to get to the next level, we're going to need a partner. A company with deep pockets and a broad geographic footprint."

Alex let his last comment settle in before proceeding.

Angie spoke first. "So you're selling the business?"

"I'm exploring the idea, yes."

Alex went on to position the sale in the context of what it would mean for Angie, Rhina, and Chris. He explained that, with the right acquirer, there would be the possibility of career advancements for each of them and that their personal objectives should become easier to meet. He also promised them each a $10,000 bonus as a thank-you if the company was sold.

The team was silent for a moment.

"Alex, I think this is a great step for you. I think we've all known for a while that you were planning to sell," said Chris.

"You did?"

"For sure," said Rhina. "You're an entrepreneur. You like the start-up and the variety. But we're beyond that stage now, and frankly, we don't need you as much anymore. Like Chris, I'm really happy for you and will do what I can to help."

"I don't think it will come as a surprise to anyone in this room that I'm ambitious," said Angie. "I would enjoy building an even bigger team and operating on a bigger playing field. I agree with Chris and Rhina—I'm happy for you and I think you're making a good decision."

Alex was stunned.

He couldn't believe how much he'd been dreading telling his management team. He felt indebted to each of them for how positively they had reacted to the news. That night, he drove home feeling ten pounds lighter.

12 The Question

Babylon had been rated one of the city's finest restaurants for three years running. Alex hadn't been there before tonight and was ushered to a small private room where his hosts were waiting. Peggy Moyles sat at a large round table flanked by two overweight men. Alex estimated they were in their late forties, although years of hard living may have made them look older than they were. He greeted Peggy and she introduced him to Alistair McGrath and Simon Tupper.

Alistair was the president of RTX Printing, the largest division of RTX Global, a billion-dollar UK-based conglomerate that owned everything from radio stations to trade shows. RTX was the second largest offset printer in the United States, and Alistair knew that becoming the largest was his ticket back to London. Simon was McGrath's head of business development.

Peggy had known Alistair for a decade, having sold him a number of small printing companies over the years. She had approached him about the Stapleton Agency opportunity and had suggested a management presentation at RTX's U.S. headquarters, but Alistair suggested dinner as a first step instead.

"A pleasure to meet you," Alistair said to Alex, revealing his strong English accent.

"Likewise," Alex responded, offering both Alistair and Simon a firm handshake.

"You're working with a true professional with Ms. Moyles," Alistair said as he gestured to Peggy. "How did you two meet?"

"A friend of mine referred Peggy."

The small talk continued. A waiter arrived and offered the group a menu and Alistair the cocktail he was craving. Alistair started with scotch and Simon ordered a Grey Goose and tonic, while Peggy and Alex ordered sparkling water for the table.

Drinks arrived, and the group ordered their meal. With the waiter out of the room for a while, Alex launched into a series of questions he had prepared for RTX. He wanted to understand RTX's ambitions for the U.S. market and how they planned to diversify further.

Alistair, more interested in the wine list, deferred to Simon to answer Alex's queries on behalf of RTX. The sommelier noticed Alistair studying the wine list and offered his services.

"I understand three of you ordered the tenderloin this evening. I suggest the 2001 White Hall Lane Cabernet. It was a great year in Napa."

"That sounds fine," Alistair said.

Alex wondered just how much a good year in Napa would cost the shareholders of RTX Global.

"Tell me a little bit about the Stapleton Agency," asked Simon.

Alex described the Five-Step Logo Design Process and his sales team as Simon and Alistair listened. Peggy stayed largely silent, letting Alex handle the questions. Steaks arrived and RTX's shareholders were stung for another bottle of White Hall Lane. Alistair concentrated on his steak, content to let Simon and Alex carry the conversation.

Plates were cleared and coffee ordered. As the waiter left the room, Alistair adjusted his chair slightly to square himself to Alex. They made eye contact and Alistair asked the only real question of the evening.

"So Alex, tell me something. Why do you want to sell your business?"

The question was so simple and obvious that Alex kicked himself for not rehearsing an answer. He had anticipated questions about his sales process, his cash flow, and profit margin, but this one simple question had him on the defensive. His heart raced and he could feel his face become flushed. He kicked himself for drinking the second glass of wine. Buying some time, he raised his napkin to his lips and pretended to wipe away some sort of offensive debris left over from dinner. Finally, he answered truthfully.

"It's been almost ten years since I started the Stapleton Agency. We've had a good run, but I'm ready to spend more time with my kids and do some traveling with my wife."

Alistair seemed satisfied with the response and turned the conversation to sports. Alex sat back and polished off the last mouthful of wine in his glass.

———◆———

The four said their good-byes on the sidewalk outside of Babylon. Alistair and Simon congratulated Alex on the success of his business and promised to get back to Peggy next week.

It was an unusually warm night for May so they walked slowly. Alex offered to escort Peggy back to her car parked a couple of blocks away.

"That seemed to go well. What do you think?" asked Alex.

"I think they're going to pass."

"What do you mean? They just said they'd be in touch next week."

"They're not interested."

"How do you know?"

"Look, I've been doing this long enough to know that dinner was just window dressing. The only question that mattered was when Alistair asked you why you want to sell your business. Once he heard your answer, the meeting was over as far as he was concerned."

Alex's mind went back to replay his answer.

"Peggy, I responded truthfully. Did you want me to lie?"

"No, I don't want you to lie, but there is a right and a wrong way to answer that question. A buyer wants to hear that you see a future for your business and you want their help to get you to the next level. They want to hear that you personally are going to stay on after the sale."

"But Peggy, I thought I was clear that I didn't want a deal with a three- to five-year earn-out. I'm willing to stay on for a while, but I want to go do something else."

"I understand, but there is a right way and a wrong way to say that."

"What do you suggest?"

"Tell them you're proud of the growth you've achieved and that you're at a point in your life where you'd like to create some liquidity for the value you've created so far *and* have an opportunity to participate in some of the future upside of the business."

"But that's not exactly true. I want to sell my business."

"I understand that, but my job is to get you the highest possible price with the largest possible percentage up front. To do that, a buyer needs to feel motivated, and to feel motivated they need to hear you're genuinely keen on tapping into their resources to help you get to the next level."

Peggy added, "Alex, buyers understand that entrepreneurs want to put some cash in their jeans, but nobody wants to buy a sinking ship where the captain is about to jump. They need to feel like you see a future for the business and that you're excited about exploiting the assets they have. They need to feel like you're willing to stay on for a period of time to help them tap into some of the synergies of the two businesses."

"How long are you suggesting?"

"We don't have to pinpoint a time frame now, but you do need to give the buyer the sense that you're willing to stay on for a transition period. Leaving it vague would be best at this point. Once you have been acquired, you'll become an employee of the acquirer and, just like any employee, it will be up to them to find a way to keep you engaged. For me to get you the best deal possible, with the most cash up front, they need to hear the things I just mentioned."

Alex drove home disappointed. He'd blown a good opportunity with RTX and was embarrassed. He'd come off like a farm league rookie and the boys from RTX played big league ball.

———— • ————

Marcus Knightsbridge adjusted his glasses and used his fingers to comb the bangs away from his eyes. Alex thought Marcus looked somewhat disheveled to be the lead business development executive for Print Technology Group.

"Alex, can you please explain your sales cycle?"

Alex, Peggy, and Marcus had been holed up in the boardroom of EMG Capital Partners for more than two hours. Print Technology Group, the third largest provider of color printers in the United States, had responded to Peggy's teaser. Like RTX, Print Technology Group thought the Stapleton Agency could supply them with a steady flow of new business leads, all of whom would want to print their new logo on one of Print Technology Group's full-color printers.

Marcus had been provided with the Book and, sufficiently impressed, requested a management presentation from the Stapleton Agency. Marcus continued to plod through his list of questions. By the fourth hour, Peggy proposed a break. It was a beautiful July day, so she took them to a French restaurant with a patio across the street from her office. Lunch was a welcome reprieve from Marcus's relentless questioning. They dined and enjoyed some relatively easy banter.

Peggy excused herself for a visit to the ladies' room, leaving Marcus and Alex alone. Marcus brought the conversation around to business and the purpose of his trip.

"Alex, it seems like you've built a great business and it's growing nicely. Out of curiosity, why do you want to sell?"

This time, Alex was prepared.

"We've proven the model can work in one city. I'm at a stage of my life personally that I'd like to create some liquidity for the value I've created so far, and I'd like to find a partner that can help us replicate the model in other cities and allow me to share in some of the future growth."

Alex was proud of himself for getting it out of his mouth without stuttering or sounding too rehearsed. His only regret was that Peggy missed his performance.

Harry arrived at the Stapleton Agency on time. He wore a blue golf shirt tucked into a pleated pair of chinos. He had managed to hike his belt so high that his waistline appeared to rest just under his rib cage. He was at the Stapleton Agency for a midyear review.

"You guys are doing really well, Alex. Your revenue for the first six months of the year was more than $2.4 million. You've already put $450,000 on the bottom line and you're only six months into the year. At this rate, you may exceed $1 million in pretax profit this year. Given where you were a couple of years ago, that's an amazing achievement."

Alex smiled and knew he was on track to deliver the year-end projections he had provided Peggy.

It had been two weeks since the Print Technology Group management presentation with Marcus, and Peggy was starting to get worried. There'd been no communication from Marcus, which seemed odd to Peggy, given how well the meeting had gone. Rather than wait for Print Technology Group, Peggy had devised a backup plan and asked Alex to join her at EMG Capital Partners for a meeting.

"Alex, I know we've been going down the road of finding you a strategic buyer like Print Technology Group, but I had an interesting lunch last week with an acquaintance from Springboard

Private Capital Partners. I told him about your business and he'd like to know more about the Stapleton Agency."

"Sounds intriguing . . ."

"We do a lot of work with Springboard, so I know how they do deals. They like investing in growing companies like the Stapleton Agency."

"Are you talking about a private equity company?"

"Yes. If they like your business, they would buy half of your company, which allows you to put some money in your pocket. Then they invest more of their cash—probably about $1 million in your case—to help you get to the next level."

"What kind of valuation would they use?"

"Springboard bought a marketing service business last year and valued the company at three to four times pretax profit."

"Sounds a little low to me. And they'd only buy half of my business and want me to stay on for another five years?" Alex said in disbelief.

"Yes, they're not operators. They're financial buyers who would inject more money into your operations and would be looking for a significant return on their investment."

Alex didn't need much time to respond. "Peggy, I'm surprised that you even consider this a possibility. You know we're a cash flow positive business. If we wanted to reinvest in the business, we'd have plenty of cash to do that now. The valuation is low and the idea of staying on for five years is a nonstarter with me."

"Fair enough. My job is to bring you all of the options, that's all."

"I understand. Any word from Print Technology Group?"

"Nothing yet."

13   A Sellable Company

The call came in on Alex's mobile. It was 7:00 p.m. and the August sun was still warm enough for him to have the sunroof open. He closed the sunroof as he answered the call.

"Hey, Alex. It's Peggy."

"What's up?"

"Good news. I think Print Technology Group is preparing an offer."

A rush of adrenaline came over Alex and he had to pull over into a gas station.

"That's great news, Peggy. Do you have any idea what they're thinking?"

"No. Marcus is a professional and wouldn't tip his hand over the phone. He's asked for some more background material on our three-year projections, which I need to get to him tomorrow. He told me he's expecting to e-mail me a letter of intent by the end of day Thursday. Why don't we plan to meet first thing on Friday morning?"

———◆———

It was 6:30 a.m. and Alex had been lying awake for more than an hour. He got up and proceeded to the Starbucks down the street from his house and ordered the usual. He had to kill an hour and a half before his meeting with Peggy was scheduled to start.

He drove wide circles around the offices of EMG Capital Partners and parked at 7:45 a.m. Peggy greeted him in the hallway. They were the first to arrive at EMG that morning, so Peggy turned on the office lights. Her body language gave away nothing of what was in the offer, despite her having read it the night before. Alex tried to look casual.

"I received a letter of intent from Print Technology Group last night."

Alex could wait no longer. "And . . . ?"

"I think you're going to like the offer," Peggy said as she handed it to him.

Alex took the document and started to read. His eyes quickly found the number. Print Technology Group was offering Alex $6 million for the Stapleton Agency. He wanted to display a calm façade for Peggy, but he could feel his face turn red with excitement. He had worked so hard to transform the Stapleton Agency and finally someone was validating his work. This little business that Alex had started from a basement office in his home ten years earlier was now worth $6 million!

Sensing that Alex needed to digest the offer, Peggy remained quiet for another minute.

"Alex, their offer is $6 million up front, plus, if you achieve the revenue and profit projections in your three-year business plan, they'll pay you another $3 million in the form of an earnout. The offer is contingent on Print Technology Group completing a sixty-day due diligence. They've asked us to give them exclusivity while they do their homework, which is pretty standard when big companies buy businesses of your size. If we want to accept the letter of intent, then we need to sign it back by September 15."

Alex left Peggy's office and called his wife to tell her the good news.

Alex sat silently as Ted read all six pages of the Print Technology Group letter of intent, making notes in the margin as he went. He turned to Alex.

"Congratulations, Alex. This is a big step for you. How do you feel?"

"I'm excited. It seems like such a long journey and we're almost there."

"Alex, this is a great offer, but we're a long way from being finished. This is a nonbinding letter of intent. They've asked for a two-month exclusivity period while they do their due diligence, and a lot can happen over the next sixty days."

Alex had fixated on the number and had not read the entire document in detail. He was somewhat disappointed that Ted wasn't sharing in his excitement.

"Ted, this *is* a great offer and Print Technology Group is a great strategic fit for us. What concerns you about the offer?"

"This is a nonbinding letter of intent. It's not the same thing as a binding offer. They can walk away from their offer at any time for any reason."

Alex looked deflated and Ted tried to cheer him up. "Don't get me wrong, Alex. This is a great milestone for you, and I think the Print Technology Group offer of six times your pretax profit this year is fair. I just don't want you to take the money to the bank yet."

Alex left Ted's office somewhat discouraged, realizing he was still a long way from selling his company.

Marcus instructed his associate David Reynolds to leave no stone unturned when investigating the Stapleton Agency.

David arrived at Alex's office early Monday morning. He adjusted his tortoiseshell glasses and swung a large briefcase over his shoulder to release a hand, which he extended to introduce himself. Alex sequestered David in his office so as not to arouse suspicion among the employees.

After some light banter, David began his interrogation.

"Alex, you claim there are fifty-eight thousand businesses in your immediate addressable market. Could you help me understand how you arrived at that number?"

Alex detailed all of the assumptions he and Ted had made in the calculation of the target market.

David was not satisfied. "I understand your math, Alex, but what I don't understand is why all of those companies would need a new logo. Isn't a logo something a company creates once?"

"A company logo is something businesses keep for a long time. That's why most of our business comes from creating product logos or new logos for spin-off divisions from companies we've worked with in the past."

"Yes, but surely companies don't create logos for each new product they launch."

"In our experience, companies create new logos for major product lines. For example, take Natural Foods. They are in the organic food business. When they decided to go into the ice cream business, they hired us to create the Natural Treats logo. They're now talking about launching a line of pet food and could need a new logo for that product line too."

"I'm sure Natural Foods is the exception," David said skeptically.

"Not really. Spring Valley Homes likes to create a new logo for each of their new development projects. We've been hired to produce three logos for Spring Valley in the last two years."

Finally, David seemed satisfied with the market size and moved on to probe Alex's process for hiring salespeople and his plans for expanding office space. David asked to see Alex's lease and a copy of every customer file. He pored over bank statements. He asked to read the Five-Step Logo Design Process instruction manual. The man had an insatiable appetite for information!

The grilling ended sometime past 5:00 p.m. Alex needed a strong drink.

The next forty-five days were among the most grueling of Alex's career. David's visit seemed to have increased his curiosity about the inner workings of the Stapleton Agency. Each line of questioning pulled a thread, which unfurled another long line of inquiries. Alex was glad to be meeting with Ted, if for no other reason than to take a break from David's incessant interrogation.

"I'm starting to lose patience with Print Technology Group," Alex said.

"I thought you liked their business development guy. What was his name, Marcus something or other?"

"Yes, Marcus Knightsbridge is all right, but he assigned a pit bull named David Reynolds to lead the due diligence process, and he just can't seem to get enough information. Every document I send him triggers a request for three more."

"Due diligence is tough. David's job is to make sure Print Technology Group doesn't buy a dud. He will keep asking questions until Marcus calls him off. It sounds like you need to apply some pressure on Marcus."

"What do you propose?" Alex asked, intrigued by Ted's suggestion.

"They've had almost two months to investigate your business and you need to force them into a decision. It's time for a little strategic table-pounding."

"Are you proposing I pitch some sort of fit?"

"Not necessarily a fit, but every negotiation reaches a point where you need to communicate to the other side that they've pushed you as far as they can. David's job is to ask questions, so Marcus needs to hear directly from you that he's in jeopardy of losing this deal."

"What makes you so sure that Marcus will care if he loses the deal?"

"Marcus would have gone to his boss for approval to make the offer to buy you. They've just spent almost two months and hundreds of hours investigating your company and they're now invested in this deal. Marcus's job is to do deals, and he is going to look silly if he wasted Print Technology Group's time with a deal that's not going ahead."

———— • ————

The phone call started off cordially enough, with Marcus giving a summary of where they were at. "David is keeping me in the loop with his work and we continue to be excited about the opportunity to bring the Stapleton Agency into the Print Technology Group family of companies."

"Thanks, Marcus. We're excited about the synergies as well, but I'm starting to get the sense you don't really want to do this deal. David has been hounding us for document after document. You've had almost two months to investigate us. If you can't make a decision based on the information you have to date, we're going to have to move on."

"Alex, I apologize if the process has been difficult. I'm sorry if we've given you the impression, at any point, that we're not interested in closing this deal. I'll check in with David and find out if there is anything else we need, but I'm fairly confident we're just about there."

"Can we agree to a closing date in the next two weeks?"

"I think that's possible. Let me check with my team and get back to you and Peggy via e-mail."

14   The Finish Line

The meeting with Print Technology Group was scheduled for Monday, November 16, at the EMG Capital Partners office. Marcus agreed to a closing date of November 30 and wanted to discuss the results of their due diligence process with Alex and Peggy in person. He got straight to business.

"Alex, we continue to be excited about the Stapleton Agency."

Alex's heart sank as the tone of Marcus's voice revealed that a "but" was about to pass his lips.

"But the due diligence process has revealed some things that we're not entirely comfortable with."

After eight weeks of due diligence and six months of work with Peggy, Print Technology Group was about to yank the deal. Peggy sensed Alex's disappointment.

Peggy asked, "What exactly are you concerned about?"

"My colleague David was not entirely comfortable with the methodology used to size the market."

Instead of engaging in a debate, Peggy asked Marcus to lay his cards on the table. "So what exactly are you saying?"

"We'd still very much like to do this deal, but the valuation model we used to arrive at the original offer in our letter of intent doesn't hold up based on the new information we gleaned from the due diligence process. As a result, we're adjusting our offer to $5.2 million up front. We're leaving the earn-out piece untouched."

Alex couldn't believe his ears. He thought they had a deal in principle. He knew himself well enough to know that he needed to leave the room before he said something he would regret.

Sensing that Alex was upset, Peggy quickly adjourned the meeting with a promise to get back to Marcus by the end of the week.

Alex spent most of Monday afternoon stalking around his office. He didn't sleep well on Monday evening, so by the time he arrived at Ted's office his nerves were frayed. He found it cathartic to rant to Ted.

"I can't believe they want to change the deal two weeks before we're supposed to close. We had a deal. I agreed to move forward based on an up-front valuation of $6 million and they're lopping more than 10 percent off the price because some weasel in a back office didn't like one of my spreadsheets."

Ted let him blow off steam. Finally, sensing Alex had calmed down, he weighed in.

"Alex, I wish I could tell you I was surprised, but I'm not."

"You knew this was going to happen?" Alex asked, directing his frustration toward Ted for the first time.

"It's very common for a company to lower their offer price after the due diligence process. They know they have you cornered and your only two choices are to accept the lower price or walk. Of the four businesses I sold, three of them closed with a lower price than was originally proposed in the letter of intent."

"I'm going to tell them to go to hell!" Alex exclaimed, still steaming about what he saw as Print Technology Group's dishonorable negotiation tactic.

"Alex, that's your right and I would understand if you chose to walk away. But before you do that, I want you to go back to your office and find the envelope I had you put in a safe place. Open it up and study it before you call Peggy."

———•———

Back at his office, Alex unlocked his desk drawer and saw the sealed envelope he had left there almost a year ago. He opened the letter and pulled out the single recipe card inside. There, written in his own handwriting, Alex saw the number he had dreamed of selling the Stapleton Agency for more than a year ago: $5,000,000.

He held the card in his hand as he gazed down at the number. He thought about all of his work over the past few years. He remembered John Stevens and how dependent they once were on MNY Bank. He thought about Elijah Kaplan, Tony Martino, and the rest of the mediocre team he had settled for to create second-rate advertising campaigns. He thought about how good Chris and his team had become at creating logos. He thought about the late-night calls to Mary Pradham and why he wanted to sell his business in the first place, and how he went about calculating his dream check.

He smiled for the first time in forty-eight hours and called Peggy to give her the news.

"I'm prepared to accept the lower offer provided Print Technology Group closes on November 30. If they stall or delay at all, I'm out."

"I think you've made a good decision, Alex. I'll call Marcus."

"Just make sure we get this done by the thirtieth."

———•———

The morning of November 30 was spent at Print Technology Group's law firm. Alex's signature was required on a variety of documents. After he was finished and the obligatory congratulations were offered, Alex excused himself. He got in his Range Rover and drove with no particular destination in mind. The trees whisked by as he reached cruising speed. Suddenly he felt the vibration of his mobile receiving an e-mail; it was a message from Mary Pradham at MNY Bank.

Alex:

   We've just received a rather large wire transfer into your personal account from Print Technology Group. Please call me when you get a chance as I'd like to give you some suggestions for investing these funds.

Alex smiled and kept driving.

How to Create a Business That Can Thrive Without You

L ike Alex Stapleton, many business owners find themselves trapped in an unsellable business. Customers ask to deal with the owner, the owner becomes personally involved in serving the customer, reinforcing the customer's reliance on the owner, and the cycle continues. A business reliant on its owner is unsellable, so the owner becomes trapped in the business.

The following eight steps provide a road map for creating a company that can thrive without you. I've also included my own personal observations and experiences gleaned from applying the process in my businesses.

Before you start this process, engage a good accountant experienced in helping business owners with succession planning. Depending on your tax jurisdiction, there will be tax-planning strategies your accountant can put into place now that will minimize your tax bill when you sell your business. *Do not wait until you have an offer to see an accountant*. Timing is critical.

STEP 1:

ISOLATE A PRODUCT OR SERVICE WITH THE POTENTIAL TO SCALE.

The first step in building a company that can thrive without you is to find a service or product that has the potential to scale. Scalable things meet three criteria: (1) They are "teachable" to employees (like the Stapleton Agency's Five-Step Logo Design Process) or can be delivered through technology; (2) they are "valuable" to your customers, which allows you to avoid commoditization; (3) they are "repeatable," meaning customers need to return again and again to buy (e.g., think razor blades, not razors).

Brainstorm all of the products and services that you provide today and plot them on a simple diagram with "Teachable" on one axis and "Valuable" on the other:

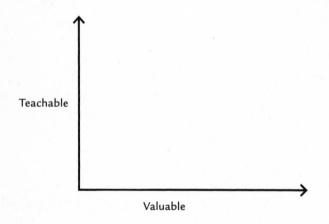

Once you have plotted everything you offer on the chart, eliminate services or products that a customer needs to buy only once.

Often, you'll find that the most teachable services or products are the ones that customers value the least. Alternatively, you'll find that the products and services your customers value most are the least teachable. That's normal. Try combining one or more services or products to create the ideal offering.

By way of a hypothetical example, let's take a look at how Alex Stapleton might have plotted his services before deciding to focus exclusively on creating logos. You'll recall he had Elijah working on the branch posters for MNY Bank. Since creating a branch poster is a simple task that lots of marketing agencies can do, Alex would have plotted the branch posters at the top left of the chart: high on teachable, since he could get his juniormost designer to do them, but also low on value to customers because branch posters can be done by lots of other marketing agencies.

You may also recall how Chris Sawchuk was struggling to get the local bicycle shop to be ranked number one on Google's natural search listings. Chris was a generalist designer without any specific knowledge of search engine optimization (SEO). In fact, SEO is a highly sought-after skill in the market that requires a deep subject matter knowledge and years of experience to do well. Successful SEO is very valuable but also very difficult to teach, which is why Alex would have plotted the SEO project for the bike shop on the bottom right corner of the chart.

On another level, creating logos was something Alex could teach his staff to execute, and since they had come up with a unique, proprietary approach to developing them that clients liked, Alex would have plotted Ziggy's Natural Treats logo at the top right of the chart.

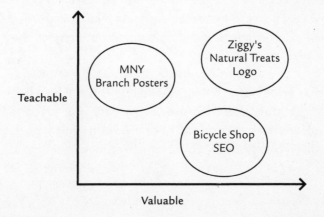

LESSONS FROM EXPERIENCE

Of the three criteria for a scalable product or service—teachable, valuable, and repeatable—I found the single most important factor in driving up the value of my companies was ensuring my revenue was repeatable, meaning customers had to repurchase somewhat regularly.

Although all recurring revenue will have a positive impact on your company's value, some forms are more desirable than others. Based on what I've learned from talking to buyers, here are six forms of recurring revenue presented from least to most valuable:

NO. 6:
CONSUMABLES—TOOTHPASTE

Consumables are disposable items customers purchase regularly but that they have no solid motivation to be brand-loyal toward.

Each morning I wake up and brush my teeth with Crest Whitening Gel. I'm fairly sure the "whitening gel" is a placebo, but it appeals to me given the amount of black coffee and red wine I consume. Every once in a while, I'll go off the beaten path and try a Colgate product that promises "extra whitening," but I always work my way back to Crest.

If you sell a consumable, start tracking your repurchase rate from existing customers. This will be a number that acquirers will use to calculate your projected sales into the future—and to calculate how much they're willing to pay to buy your company today.

NO. 5:
SUNK MONEY CONSUMABLES—RAZOR BLADES

More valuable than basic consumables such as tooth-paste are "sunk money consumables." In the case of these items, the customer has made an investment in a platform.

When I started using Gillette Sensor razor blades, I first had to buy a handle. Now I buy a new five-pack of blades every month, and I can't bring myself to try Schick because then I'd have to purchase its handle mechanism. I've been a Sensor guy since I grew my first patch of peach fuzz. I've made an investment in the plat-form, and that makes me reluctant to switch providers.

The same is true at the office. When I was in the market for a printer, I bought a Xerox. And even though I probably won't need to buy another printer for a while, I still have to buy Xerox's expensive toner cartridges.

Expect to garner a premium for your business if you can demonstrate a loyal group of customers who have made an investment in your platform.

NO. 4:
RENEWABLE SUBSCRIPTIONS—MAGAZINES

Even better than having loyal customers who repurchase is having revenue that is guaranteed into the future. For example, I am a loyal subscriber to *Outside* magazine. Each year I get a re-up letter, and I send a check to cover my next twelve issues. *Outside* recognizes one-twelfth of my subscription fee the month it receives the check and each of the next eleven months.

Magazines are cheap compared with the subscrip-tions that analyst firms such as Frost & Sullivan or IDC sell their customers, which can run into the hundreds of thousands of dollars, making these companies more valuable than their competitors that offer project-based consulting on a one-off basis.

NO. 3:
SUNK MONEY RENEWABLE SUBSCRIPTIONS—
THE BLOOMBERG TERMINAL

When customers make an investment to do business with you, they become very sticky. If they buy on a subscription model, you will have one of the most valuable businesses in your industry.

Traders and money managers swear by their Bloomberg Terminal. Bloomberg customers have to first buy or lease the terminal and then subscribe to Bloomberg's financial information. Having sticky customers loyal to a proprietary platform allowed Michael Bloomberg to build a valuable company.

NO. 2:
AUTO-RENEWAL SUBSCRIPTIONS—
DOCUMENT STORAGE

When you store documents with Iron Mountain, you are charged a fee each month until you ask for your documents to be shredded or you agree to pick them up. Unlike a magazine subscription, for which you have to make the conscious decision to re-up, Iron Mountain just bills you until you tell it to stop.

Iron Mountain tracks its cancellation rate down to the decimal point and it can predict its revenue well into the future, which is why it is such a valuable company.

NO. 1:
CONTRACTS—WIRELESS PHONES

The only thing more valuable than an automatic renewal subscription is a hard contract for a defined term.

As much as we may despise being tied to them, wireless companies have mastered the art of recurring revenue. Many give their customers free phones as long as the customer locks into a two- or three-year full-service contract.

As you ascend the recurring-revenue hierarchy, expect the value of your business to go up in lockstep.

Once you've isolated what is teachable, what your customers value, and what they need most often, document your process for delivering this type of product or service. You'll recall Ted helping Alex to define and document the Five-Step Logo Design Process. As Ted explained, describe each of the steps so that you can repeat the model in the same way each time. This will form the basis of your instruction manual for delivering that product or service. Use examples and fill-in-the-blank templates where possible to help ensure that your instructions are specific enough for someone to follow independently. Test your instructions by asking a team or team member to deliver the service or product without your involvement. Getting the instruction manual right will require time and patience. Expect to develop many drafts.

Next, name your scalable product or service. Naming your offering gives you ownership of it and helps you differentiate it from those of potential competitors. Once you own something unique, you move from providing a commoditized service or product to providing one whose terms of use you decide. If your product or service isn't generic, customers won't be able to compare your price to others'. Instead, name your offering, along with each of the steps you take to deliver it, to differentiate your offer so that you can set its price and payment terms.

After you come up with a great name, write a short description of the features and corresponding benefits of each step in the production of your offering. Revamp all of your customer communications (e.g., Web site, brochure) to describe your process in a uniform way.

LESSONS FROM EXPERIENCE

I used to own a marketing services business that provided focus groups. You know the drill—the clients are sipping beer on one side of the one-way mirror while eight hapless "respondents" on the other provide their feedback on whatever the client wants to peddle.

Focus groups used to be a great business. It cost about $2,500 per group to rent a facility and pay the respondents. We would charge $6,000 for each group and clear a tidy $3,500, or roughly 58 percent gross margin. I say "used to be a great business" because as other companies caught on to the profitability of focus groups, the competition increased, driving down prices. Worse, clients started to issue requests for proposals (RFPs) for their focus groups.

The first time I saw an RFP, I was excited. The client was a big phone company, and it had asked our little company for a proposal to conduct six focus groups. A $36,000 potential order was a big deal for us, so I painstakingly responded to all of the RFP's questions. I sent off my proposal and waited. Eventually I got a call from the phone company saying it had chosen another bidder. I couldn't believe it. I'd thought my proposal was perfect.

I followed up with the buyer, and after several failed

attempts finally reached him and demanded an explanation. He told me the winning bid was $3,500 per group. I would have had to drop my gross margin to $1,000 per group, or 29 percent! I would have had only twenty-nine measly points to pay for all of my operating expenses such as payroll, rent, and so on.

If you want your business to be profitable, enjoy fat margins, and thrive without you, you need to stop responding to RFPs and start carving out your own one-of-a-kind product or service. RFPs commoditize a category down to the point where the only way for a business to win a contract is to be the lowest-cost provider.

In my business, I decided to develop an alternative to focus groups that I could control the pricing for. We called them "customer advisory boards." A company that wanted consistent and candid feedback from its customers could hire us to set up and run an annual advisory board on its behalf. We documented the process, developed an uneditable PDF deck for our salespeople to use to pitch the service, and, since customer advisory boards were unique in the market, set the price at a point where the gross margin returned to our historical averages.

STEP 2:
CREATE A POSITIVE CASH FLOW CYCLE

You'll recall that Alex Stapleton found it hard to make the big strategic changes Ted was recommending, in part because he was simultaneously fretting about having enough money in the bank to pay his employees.

By creating a positive cash flow cycle, you'll have the financial cushion—and confidence—to make some of the difficult changes required in steps 3 and 4. To create a positive cash flow cycle, charge your customer in full or in part for your product or service before you pay the costs of whatever it is you provide. For example, when you subscribe to a magazine, you send the magazine company your check and then, a few weeks later, you receive the first of a year's worth of magazines. The magazine company gets to use your money (along with that of its other subscribers) all year to hire writers, editors, and photographers to produce the magazine.

Charging up front for your product or service will be possible if you have documented and differentiated your unique offering properly (step 1). Depending on your service or product, you may not be able to charge the entire amount in advance, but try to get at least some portion of your money before delivery.

A positive cash flow cycle will also increase the value of your company. When an acquirer buys your company, he or she needs to write two checks. One, obviously, is to you, the owner(s); the second check is to your company to fund its working capital—the money required for your business to pay its day-to-day bills. If your business needs lots of cash, the acquirer will have to set aside money for working capital, lessening his or her appetite to write you a fat check. The inverse is also true: If your company generates excess cash, an acquirer will usually pay more for your business because he or she doesn't have to commit funds to working capital.

LESSONS FROM EXPERIENCE

I was driving home when I got the call I had been expecting from the mergers and acquisitions firm I was using to sell my company. I pulled over—this conversation was going to require some focus.

"We have two offers we'd like to meet to discuss," said my banker.

My pulse leaped as I tried to contain myself. "Meet?!" I said anxiously. I didn't want to wait any longer to find out what my business was worth in the eyes of an acquirer. "Are you kidding me? What are they offering?"

My advisers went on to describe the only number I cared about at the time: the purchase price the acquirers were offering to buy my business.

I didn't realize how naive I was until I sat down with my accountant, who dissected both offers. At first blush, Offer A looked like the better of the two because the purchase price was higher. My accountant, however, encouraged me to look more carefully at Offer B. Offer B included a detailed description of how the buyer would calculate the working capital I was required to leave in the company at closing.

When I first read the paragraph about working capital, I glossed over it, assuming it was irrelevant MBA-speak. Truth be told, I didn't really know what working capital meant. I had a vague notion that it had something to do with the money we needed to keep in the bank to pay for things, but I certainly didn't think it made much difference to the relative merits of each offer. My accountant explained that, given the way the potential purchaser was offering to calculate working capital, Offer B was allowing me to withdraw most of the money we had accumulated in our bank account before the deal closed—and since we charged our customers up front, we had built up a significant amount of cash. The working capital calculation in Offer B had the effect of raising the value by more than 15 percent, making it at least as good as Offer A.

If you get an offer to buy your company, the second most important number on the page may be the working capital calculation. If your offer does not include details on the working capital calculation, be sure to lock that number down before you agree to anything.

STEP 3:
HIRE A SALES TEAM

Once you have created and packaged your offering and started to charge up front, you need to remove yourself from selling it. If you have others delivering the product or service but you're still the rainmaker, you will not be able to sell your business without a long and risky earn-out.

LESSONS FROM EXPERIENCE

In 2002, on the executive education campus of MIT, I learned that I had been selling the wrong product.

I, along with sixty-one other entrepreneurs, had been going to MIT for three years to learn how to be better company builders. The program was called "The Birthing of Giants," and we had been selected from a pool of applicants who all met the same criteria: own a company with at least $1 million in annual sales and be under the age of forty.

In the final year of the program, Stephen Watkins, an entrepreneur who had recently sold his business, came to the campus to speak.

Watkins began by canvassing the room to see how

many of us were involved in selling our product or service to our customers. I, along with virtually every other entrepreneur in the room, raised my hand.

With that, he proceeded to scold us all for spending too much time selling our products and virtually no time selling our company. He went further, and I'll try to paraphrase his message for you: "Your job as an entrepreneur is to hire salespeople to sell your products and services so you can spend your time selling your company. You make a few hundred or thousand dollars when you sell your product, but if you turned those same skills to selling your company, you can make exponentially more. You have the right skills, but you're selling the wrong product."

His message landed on me with blunt force. I felt like an amateur who had gotten a glimpse at a professional game and realized the pros were playing with an entirely different set of rules. Here I was spinning my wheels selling our services when I should have been marketing my company.

From that day forward, the way I thought about my role changed. I started hiring salespeople to call on customers. At first I missed the adrenaline rush of personally making a big sale, but in time I came to enjoy seeing other people make sales even more.

I still went out on sales calls, but they were to people I thought might one day buy my company, not my product.

As you build your sales team, look for people like Angie Thacker who, first, enjoy selling and, second, like the product. Avoid hiring salespeople who come from professional services companies; they will likely want to reinvent your product or service for every customer. If at all possible, hire at least two people to do sales, not just one. For one thing, sales careers typically attract competitive people, and a little healthy competition between these employees will work in your favor; for another, an acquirer will want to see that you have a product or service that can be sold by salespeople in general and not just one superstar salesperson.

LESSONS FROM EXPERIENCE

In the early days of my market research company, I churned through salespeople. Despite my spending hours coaching them and offering plenty of incentives for success, most struggled to hit whatever measly quota I gave them. By contrast, I was consistently able to sell our services. I met with customers, tried to listen to their needs, and went back to them with ideas to fix whatever ailed them. More often than not, they bought what I was selling. It seemed easy, making it all the more frustrating that I couldn't hire salespeople to replace me.

In retrospect, it wasn't that I was a superstar salesperson and my team was made up of underperformers. I had simply invested more time learning the market research profession than they had. Like most business owners, in the early days I did both the selling and the doing, so I had executed all kinds of research projects and had made many mistakes, and consequently I'd built a base of understanding around what worked and what didn't. When I did the selling, I was subconsciously relying on seven years of experience in market research.

My salespeople were being asked to talk intelligently about a wide variety of research services that they couldn't possibly know everything about. Meanwhile, I was thrashing around grasping for revenue anywhere I could find it and tailoring our services for every customer who asked. All of my zigzagging and customization undermined my salespeople; they were like police officers trying to trail a drunk driver.

It wasn't until we stopped selling 90 percent of what we were offering in favor of a single subscription of reports and events (step 1) that I was actually able to get salespeople to start making sales. With less to sell, my salespeople were able to master one kind of market research. Again, it wasn't that they all of a sudden became knowledgeable researchers; they simply got a chance to repeatedly practice a single pitch.

STEP 4:
STOP SELLING EVERYTHING ELSE

Once you've assembled a great sales team, stop taking on projects that fall outside of the standard offering you identified in step 1. It's tempting to accept these sales because they bolster your revenue and cash flow. If you're charging up front for your service or product and your salespeople are selling it, then you shouldn't have to worry about cash flow. That leaves added revenue as the reason to accept projects that fall outside of your process. The revenue may feel good at first, but it comes at an unacceptable cost: Your team will lose focus; customers, realizing that you're not serious about your standard process, will see a chink in your armor and start asking for customization of their projects; and to meet this demand, you will need to hire other people to deliver.

I've had the opportunity to speak with hundreds of business owners who have made this transition, and most have told me that customers who used to ask for custom services respected the change they'd made to their business model. Many clients actually buy more once the service or product is standardized. Customers are smart; they often know you're overreaching your capabilities in accepting assignments that fall outside of your sweet spot.

Stopping yourself from accepting projects outside of your scalable product or service is the toughest part of creating a business that can thrive without you. You will have employees testing your resolve and customers asking for exceptions, and you will second-guess yourself on more than one occasion. This is normal; you have to be strong on this and resist the temptation. There is a point where the wind will start blowing the other way and your customers, employees, and stakeholders will finally realize that you're serious about focusing on one thing. It takes time. It will happen, and when it does and you feel as if the boat has actually shifted, you will have sailed a long way toward creating a sellable company.

LESSONS FROM EXPERIENCE

Business owners often believe that to be "customer-centric," they have to give customers whatever they want. But giving customers too much choice can be a detriment, especially if you're trying to build a company you can scale and ultimately sell. I learned this the hard way.

It all started after I read a glowing article about Jupiter Research (now part of Forrester), a consulting firm that provided research studies to customers through a subscription offering. Jupiter would do one piece of research and present it to all of its customers. Finally, I thought, a model that could bring some scale and leverage to my consulting business.

I spent the next weekend plotting how to shift my consulting firm to a similar model. I decided that my company would publish six major research reports each year with an annual subscription price of $50,000. It would cost a single company more than that to commission one report, but now the company would be getting a total of six reports—a good deal for the customer, I reasoned. And at $50,000 per subscription, all we needed was one hundred subscribers to have a $5 million business. A good deal for us too.

I divided our prospects into A, B, and C leads. The As were our long-terms clients, Bs were sporadic customers, and Cs were people we'd never met. Interestingly, the plan sold best with B customers. They knew us better than the Cs but were not so entrenched with us that they viewed a cookie-cutter offering as a step back in our relationship.

The problem was, I burned through our B customers quickly. I managed to get seventeen subscribers, which amounted to $850,000 on an annual basis. A nice chunk of revenue to be sure, but not enough to make it worth walking away from our other clients. If I was going to make the subscription model fly, I would need to convince my A customers to join the seventeen Bs who had already committed.

However, my As simply weren't interested in the subscription. Some thought they were giving us so much consulting work that we should throw in the subscription free as a thank-you for their business. Others didn't like the model's cookie-cutter nature. Each time I met with my A customers, I would listen carefully to their feedback and invariably assure them that they could continue to do business with us using the old model. And that was my mistake. Giving our A clients the choice ensured that they would never make the move to the subscription offering. Our *A* customers had become *As* because we were providing value to their business, and they didn't want to mess with a formula that worked for them.

So I ran the subscription program while at the same time continuing our consulting business. Things went downhill quickly. Client deadlines and demands eventually overshadowed the subscription business, and the quality of the reports suffered. Employees preferred to work on custom consulting projects instead of writing formulaic reports. I felt as though I were trying to take off with an overloaded plane—I could get the front wheels off the ground but didn't have enough torque to get the heavy plane airborne.

As I got more desperate for *A* clients to make the switch, I made a second mistake, which would ultimately be fatal: I started offering to customize each report for my *A* customers if they agreed to move to the new subscription model. Once our staff got wind that one subscriber was getting a special report, all of our account managers wanted their customers to have the very best reports for them. I fell down the slippery slope of customizations quickly. Soon we were customizing each report for every client—thereby compromising the leverage I'd hoped to achieve through a subscription model.

It wasn't long before things started spiraling out of control. With six major studies per year and seventeen clients demanding special reports, we faced the prospect of creating 102 unique reports—untenable for our twenty employees. Finally, mired in requests for customization and tired of the difficulties of running two different types of business in parallel, I shut down the subscription business.

Over the following five years, I concluded that my two biggest mistakes were: (1) giving my *A* clients the choice to continue to do business with us under the old model, and (2) customizing the reports of those who did agree to make the switch. I decided to relaunch a version of the program but forced our customers to make a choice: Either subscribe to our standard subscription or end our business relationship. Giving customers an ultimatum actually worked in most cases, and we quickly made up for lost consulting revenue with new *A* subscribers. We got more focused on the offer and the *A*s and *B*s started talking it up, so we received more inbound leads from *C*s. The business really started to take off, and, better yet, it was scalable. All because we led and didn't follow our customers.

Once you have weaned yourself off other projects, you need to operate your newly focused business for at least two years in order to prove to a buyer that your new model works.

Over the course of these two years, drive the model as far and fast as you can. Avoid the temptation to get personally involved in selling or delivering your standard offering. Instead, when you get asked for help, diagnose the problem and fix your system so the problem doesn't recur.

Many business owners realize a tremendous uptick in their quality of life in these two years. Business improves, cash flows, and customer headaches decrease. In fact, many owners like this stage so much, they shelve their plans to sell their company and decide to run it in perpetuity. If this happens to you, congratulations. If you still want to sell your business, continue on to the next step.

STEP 5:

LAUNCH A LONG-TERM INCENTIVE PLAN FOR MANAGERS

If you'd like to have a business you could sell, you need to prove to a buyer that you have a management team who can run the business after you're gone. What's more, you need to show that the management team is locked into staying with your company after acquisition.

Avoid using equity to retain key management through an acquisition, as it will unnecessarily complicate the sale process and dilute your holdings. Instead, create a long-term incentive plan for your key managers. Each year, take an amount equivalent to their annual bonus and put it aside in a long-term incentive account earmarked for each manager you want to retain. Allow the manager to withdraw one-third of the account's balance each year after a three-year period. That way, a good manager must always walk away from a significant amount of money should he or she decide to leave your company.

You may also choose to "top up" the balance in a long-term incentive plan with a one-time special bonus in the event of the sale of your business. That way, your key managers will have an increased incentive to help you sell your business *and* stay with your company after the sale to get their share of the proceeds.

Visit www.BuiltToSell.com to find a template for a long-term incentive plan.

LESSONS FROM EXPERIENCE

When I owned my marketing services company, I brought in a general manager—let's call him Jim—to run the day-to-day business operations. Over time, Jim proved himself to be a reliable manager. He was good with clients and could deal with the administrative side of running our business.

I had not yet discovered the long-term incentive plan technique for retaining key staff, so instead I gave him a good salary and a share of our profits each year. Jim was doubly motivated to increase our pretax profit because I gave him 12 percent of whatever profit we generated below $200,000 and 20 percent of every dollar we generated above $200,000.

As the primary shareholder, I was thrilled when Jim delivered larger profits year after year. He was earning 20 percent of every dollar we made, but I was making 80 percent. What's more, Jim was so good that I was able to step away from some of the daily operations and take vacations for the first time in years. Profits and cash kept rolling in, and my stress level diminished.

Then one day I decided to sell the company. I didn't tell Jim.

As I prepared the company for sale, I started to learn about what would make an acquirer willing to pay more for my business, and I was told that buyers want standardized, long-term contracts with customers. I explained to Jim that I wanted to get all of our clients to sign a long-term contract and that I thought we should be willing to offer them a discount in return for their commitment. The discount would cut into our profitability for the year—and therefore Jim's bonus. Understandably, Jim wasn't keen on the idea, and we both dug in our heels.

Increasingly, we found ourselves on opposite sides of just about every decision, from building a new Web site to compensating our salespeople: Jim wanted what would increase our annual profit, and I wanted to focus on what would increase our value in the market—which was related to profits but not always exactly aligned. Things went from bad to worse as Jim started to shut me out of client relationships. He turned employees against me, and we became a fractured company with some staff loyal to me, others to Jim. He was a superb performer when our goals were aligned, but as my goals changed and we became misaligned, the same things that had made Jim an outstanding performer—tenacity, drive, and passion—made him a formidable thorn in my side.

Eventually, Jim and I agreed to part ways and I had to postpone my plans to sell the business by a year while I rebuilt the relationships with my clients and employees. I felt as though I had squandered an opportunity.

After my experience with Jim, I started to use a long-term incentive plan for key managers. This plan had my most valued employees taking a longer-term view of the financial rewards associated with their job, and ultimately they worked with me, not against me, as I set my business up for sale.

STEP 6:
FIND A BROKER

The next step in the process is to find representation. If your company has less than $2 million in sales, a business broker will best serve you. If it has more than $2 million in sales, a boutique mergers and acquisitions firm is probably your best bet. Look for a firm with experience in your industry, as it will already know many of the potential buyers for your business. To find an M&A firm or business broker, ask for recommendations from other entrepreneurs you know who have sold their companies.

Your broker should appreciate what you have done to transform your business. If he or she considers you to be the same as the commoditized service providers in your industry, move on. Your broker needs to recognize that you have created something special and deserve to be compensated at a higher rate.

Once you have an M&A firm or broker engaged, he or she will work with you to create "the Book" or to populate an "online data room." This information describes your business and its performance to date along with spelling out a business plan for the future.

Brokers typically charge a percentage of the proceeds of the deal in the form of a success fee.

LESSONS FROM EXPERIENCE

When I finally got serious about wanting to sell my events business, I asked around about how the process worked. I soon discovered that there are people who make a living selling and buying businesses. As I dug deeper, I found out most brokers specialize in a specific industry. I narrowed my list down to four companies, all located in New York, that specialized in selling conference businesses.

I had a warm introduction to three of the firms, so I was able to get face-to-face meetings. The fourth did not respond to my e-mail, which I found curious but would later learn was not uncommon.

I spent the day in Manhattan interviewing intermediaries, or perhaps I should say they interviewed me. Investment bankers only make any real money if the business actually gets sold, so they grilled me to ensure I had a sellable business:

- "Describe your sales cycle."

- "How many salespeople do you have?"

- "Describe your cash flow cycle."

- "Who are your customers?"

- "How do you know if they are satisfied?"

- "How often do they repurchase?"

My last meeting of the day was the most memorable. The banker on the other side of the table looked uninterested as he began asking his stock set of questions. His mood began to warm with each of my answers, to the point where his face actually broke into a broad smile as he finally interrupted me: "I know just the company to buy your business."

My reaction to his proclamation was a mixture of excitement and skepticism. After all, we had only just met. I asked him to elaborate, and he described a large company he knew well that wanted to get further into the events business in North America—he thought it was a perfect marriage. He explained that he would charge me 5 percent of the transaction value and that I would have to promise to work exclusively with his firm as my broker. I agreed to his terms, and my newfound banker friend arranged a dinner in one of Manhattan's most exclusive restaurants for us to meet the division president of the company he thought should buy my business.

As I walked into the restaurant a few minutes early for our 7 p.m. reservation, I found my banker and the division head sitting at the bar. The lads looked as if they were old friends. My guess was that they were already onto their second scotch and soda, which I found strange given that my broker was supposed to be representing me. He seemed awfully chummy with the person he would soon be negotiating against. As the evening progressed, it became clear to me that my banker and the division president were actually long-term colleagues who had done many deals together. In fact, my banker earned the majority of his fees from buying companies on behalf of his dinner guest, not by selling them.

My adviser was simply trying to deliver me as a gift to his friend. If successful, he would earn a quick fee from me and ingratiate himself further with his main client, who would have been given a first look at my business without any competition at the table to drive up the price. I left dinner far more knowledgeable about the whole process but minus a broker. The next day, I set out to find myself another—one who would be working for me.

STEP 7:
TELL YOUR MANAGEMENT TEAM

Once your broker has found a prospective buyer, he or she will set up management presentations for you and your team. At this point you will need to confide to your key managers that you are considering selling your business.

Telling your management team can be a daunting task. Think about it from their perspective and make sure there is something in it for them if the deal goes through. An acquisition can often mean significant career opportunities for your managers, and that may be enough. Nevertheless, an acquisition can be disruptive and unsettling for them, so I recommend you offer key employees a simple success bonus deposited into their long-term incentive plan (see step 5) if a deal goes through. As an added bonus, a potential acquirer will value your putting a deal-related incentive in place for your key employees to stay.

LESSONS FROM EXPERIENCE

Whenever you sell people's time, you become beholden to your employees as their expertise increases and their client relationships deepen. Like installing wheels under your most precious pallet of inventory, the better they become at their job, the more likely your best people are to roll out the door. It's one of the reasons service firm owners typically dilute themselves into nothing more than a collective of highly paid employees and rarely get acquired for much more than a long and grueling earn-out for the principals.

Warren Buffett talks about the depth and breadth of the "moat" around the businesses he invests in. A big moat gives you pricing power against your competition, but it also makes it harder for employees to leave you and set up shop as a competitor.

If all you're selling is time, the moment an employee is fully trained and meeting independently with clients, he or she becomes a flight risk and a potential liability. If you have a deep and wide moat, employees will need to invest significant time or money to build what you have created and they will realize there is more to your business than marking up their time.

In my research company, we set out to own the de facto conference in our industry. By owning the most important trade show in our space—one that both companies and vendors wanted to attend—we created a moat that was hard for a single employee to replicate. In fact, I did have one employee leave to set up a competitive shop despite having signed a noncompete agreement. She claimed to offer the same service we did, but we had a five-year head start on creating the "go-to" conference for the industry. More than just hawking hours, we had a moat that proved more than difficult for a single former employee to re-create.

Wondering what your moat could be to protect you against employee defection? Here are a few ideas to get you thinking:

- Own the annual ranking study for your category: Interbrand does the ranking of brand equity among marketers, making it tough for a one-person brand consultancy shop to compete.

- Own the annual awards program for your category: Ernst & Young created the Entrepreneur of the Year awards program, and it has solidified its position with fast-growth entrepreneurs, which gives the company a real advantage over a disgruntled former employee who hangs out his or her shingle at tax time.

- Own the event for your industry. New York–based investment banking company Allen & Co. organizes the annual gathering of media and technology executives at Sun Valley, Idaho.

- Own the benchmark: Fred Reichheld is the founder of Bain's loyalty practice and the creator of the Net Promoter Score methodology as a way to predict repurchase and referrals for businesses. His firm owns the database of benchmarks. Companies using the Net Promoter Score want to know where they stand with other companies, so they go to Bain for the benchmarks and strategy for implementing a loyalty program. Bain has a barrier to entry that would take years and many millions of dollars for a single aggrieved employee to replicate.

STEP 8:
CONVERT OFFER(S) TO A BINDING DEAL

Once you have completed your management presentations, you will, you hope, get some offers in the form of a nonbinding letter of intent (LOI). A letter of intent is not a firm offer. Unless it includes a breakup fee (rare for smaller companies), the buyer has every right to walk. In fact, deals often fall through in the due diligence period (discussed below), so don't be surprised if it happens to you.

As you review the LOI, keep in mind that your adviser will be trying to sell the benefits of the offer to you because he or she (1) will get paid if the deal goes through and (2) wants to justify the steep advisory fee by reminding you of the hard work he or she has done. Do not be swayed by your adviser. Study the offer. It will likely contain an amount of money (or some other currency, like stock) up front, with another chunk tied to one or more performance targets for your business after the sale, often referred to as an earn-out. Treat the earn-out portion as gravy. *An earn-out is used by an acquirer to minimize his or her risk in buying your company.* This means that you take most of the risk, and the buyer gets most of the reward. Some earn-outs have proven lucrative for the owners who accepted them; most business owners who have sold a business, however, have a nightmare story to share about an overbearing parent company not delivering on what was promised in an earn-out contract. As long as you get what you want for the business up front and treat the earn-out as gravy, you can walk when things get nasty. If you feel as though you have to stay to get full value for the business, then expect life to be uncomfortable for the duration of the earn-out.

The due diligence period, spelled out in the LOI, usually lasts from sixty to ninety days. A veteran entrepreneur I know likes to refer to it as the entrepreneur's "proctology exam." It isn't fun, and the best strategy is often just to survive it. Due diligence can make you feel vulnerable and exposed. A professional buyer will dispatch a team of MBA-types to your office who will quickly identify the weak spots in your model. That's their job. Try to keep your cool during this period, and try to present things in the best possible light, but do not lie or hide the facts.

LESSONS FROM EXPERIENCE

Most professional acquirers will have a checklist of questions they need answered before buying your company. They'll want answers to detailed questions like the following:

> When does your lease expire and what are the terms?

> Do you have consistent, signed, up-to-date contracts with your customers and employees?

> Are your ideas, products, and processes protected by patent or trademark?

> What kind of technology do you use, and are your software licenses up-to-date?

> What are the loan covenants on your credit agreements?

How are your receivables? Do you have any late payers or deadbeat customers?

Does your business require a license to operate, and if so, is your paperwork in order?

Do you have any litigation pending?

In addition to these objective questions, they'll try to get a subjective sense of your business. In particular, they will try to determine just how integral you are personally to the success of your business and if it is possible for your business to grow without you. Subjectively assessing how dependent the business is on you requires the buyer to do some investigative work. It's more art than science and often requires a potential buyer to use a number of tricks of the trade:

Trick #1: Juggling calendars. By asking to make a last-minute change to your meeting time, an acquirer gets clues as to how involved you are personally in serving customers. If you can't accommodate the change request, the acquirer may probe to find out why and try to determine what part of your business is so dependent on you that you have to be there.

Trick #2: Checking to see if your business is vision impaired. An acquirer may ask you to explain your vision for the business, which is a question you should be well prepared to answer. However, he or she may ask the same question of your employees and key managers. If your staff members offer inconsistent answers, the acquirer may take it as a sign that the future of the business lives only in your head.

Trick #3: Asking your customers why they do business with you. A potential acquirer may ask to talk to some of your customers. He or she will expect you to select your most passionate and loyal customers and therefore will expect to hear good things. However, the customers may be asked a question like, "Why do you do business with these guys?" The acquirer is trying to figure out where your customers' loyalties lie. If your customers answer by describing the benefits of your product, service, or company in general, that's good. If they respond by explaining how much they like you personally, that's bad.

Trick #4: Mystery shopping. Acquirers often conduct their first bit of research behind your back, before you even know they are interested in buying your business. They may pose as a customer, visit your Web site, or come into your company to understand what it feels like to be one of your customers. Make sure the experience your company offers a stranger is tight and consistent, and try to avoid personally being involved in finding or serving brand-new customers. If any potential acquirers see you personally as the key to wooing new customers, they'll be concerned that business will dry up when you leave.

Once the due diligence period is over, there is a good chance that the offer in the letter of intent will be discounted. Again, don't be surprised if this happens to you. Expect it, and you'll be pleasantly surprised if it doesn't happen. You'll need to go back to the math you did when reviewing the letter of intent in the first place. If the discounted offer meets your target cash up front, then go ahead and sign your business over. If the discounted offer falls below the threshold, walk away—no matter what the acquirer promises to help you hit your earn-out.

If you accept the revised offer or the due diligence period ends, you'll have a closing meeting. Typically held at the acquirer's law firm, this is where the formalities are handled. You sign a lot of documents, and once the documents are signed, the law firm will move the cash portion of the sale from their account to yours. The deal is done.

Summary of Ted's Tips

TED'S TIP #1

Don't generalize; specialize. If you focus on doing one thing well and hire specialists in that area, the quality of your work will improve and you will stand out among your competitors.

TED'S TIP #2

Relying too heavily on one client is risky and will turn off potential buyers. Make sure that no one client makes up more than 15 percent of your revenue.

TED'S TIP #3

Owning a process makes it easier to pitch and puts you in control. Be clear about what you're selling, and potential customers will be more likely to buy your product.

TED'S TIP #4

Don't become synonymous with your company. If buyers aren't confident that your business can run without you in charge, they won't make their best offer.

TED'S TIP #5

Avoid the cash suck. Once you've standardized your service, charge up front or use progress billing to create a positive cash flow cycle.

TED'S TIP #6

Don't be afraid to say no to projects. Prove that you're serious about specialization by turning down work that falls outside your area of expertise. The more people you say no to, the more referrals you'll get to people who need your product or service.

TED'S TIP #7

Take some time to figure out how many pipeline prospects will likely lead to sales. This number will become essential when you go to sell because it allows the buyer to estimate the size of the market opportunity.

TED'S TIP #8

Two sales reps are always better than one. Usually naturally competitive types, sales reps will try to outdo each other. And having two on staff will prove to a buyer that you have a scalable sales model, not just one good sales rep.

TED'S TIP #9

Hire people who are good at selling products, not services. These people will be better able to figure out how your product can meet a client's needs rather than agreeing to customize your offering to fit what the client wants.

TED'S TIP #10

Ignore your profit-and-loss statement in the year you make the switch to a standardized offering even if it means you and your employees will have to forgo a bonus that year. As long as your cash flow remains consistent and strong, you'll be back in the black in no time.

TED'S TIP #11

You need at least two years of financial statements reflecting your use of the standardized offering model before you sell your company.

TED'S TIP #12

Build a management team and offer them a long-term incentive plan that rewards their personal performance and loyalty.

TED'S TIP #13

Find an adviser for whom you will be neither their largest nor their smallest client. Make sure they know your industry.

TED'S TIP #14

Avoid an adviser who offers to broker a discussion with a single client. You want to ensure there is competition for your business and avoid being used as a pawn for your adviser to curry favor with his or her best client.

TED'S TIP #15

Think big. Write a three-year business plan that paints a picture of what is possible for your business. Remember, the company that acquires you will have more resources for you to accelerate your growth.

TED'S TIP #16

If you want to be a sellable, product-oriented business, you need to use the language of one. Change words like "clients" to "customers" and "firm" to "business." Rid your Web site and customer-facing communications of any references that reveal you used to be a generic service business.

TED'S TIP #17

Don't issue stock options to retain key employees after an acquisition. Instead, use a simple stay bonus that offers the members of your management team a cash reward if you sell your company. Pay the reward in two or more installments only to those who stay so that you ensure your key staff stays on through the transition.

Recommended Reading and Resources

SIGN UP AT BUILTTOSELL.COM

Each week I share my latest suggestions for building a valuable—sellable—company that can thrive without you. Sign up at www.BuiltToSell.com and instantly get access to *The Freedom Manifest*, a free e-book for business owners. We can also connect through my Twitter feed @JohnWarrillow.

Find out what your company is worth today. Take the free ten-question Sellability Index Quiz today and find out how much you could sell your business for today. www.BuiltToSell.com/quiz.

COMPLETE THE CIRCLE OF ENTREPRENEURIAL LIFE

As you prepare to exit your business, please consider helping a new entrepreneur enter the world of entrepreneurship by joining our Kiva lending team. Kiva enables you to lend small amounts of money (loans start at $25) to entrepreneurs in the developing world. Learn more about our Kiva lending team at www.BuiltToSell.com/kiva.

JOIN THE STRATEGIC COACH

The folks at Strategic Coach are the gurus on building a company and a life. They created the concept of a standard offering, which they call a unique process. They will help you articulate and implement your process. www.strategiccoach.com.

READ *THE E-MYTH* AND GET AN E-MYTH COACH

Michael Gerber coined the term "working *on* the business not *in* the business" in his bestseller *The E-Myth Revisited*. But don't just read the book; get yourself into one of the E-Myth coaching programs. www.e-myth.com.

FOLLOW TIM FERRISS

Timothy Ferriss wrote *The 4-Hour Workweek* and will have you spinning on what to do with your time after you have sold your company. www.fourhourworkweek.com.

ATTEND ANY EVENT PRODUCED BY VERNE HARNISH

Verne Harnish runs Gazelles and is the author of *Mastering the Rockefeller Habits*. He's a growth guru and his company specializes in educating and coaching growth companies. Make sure to sign up for his must-read Weekly Insights. www.gazelles.com.

READ *SMALL GIANTS*

Bo Burlingham has chronicled the entrepreneurial life for years in the pages of *Inc.* magazine. *Small Giants* will inspire you to focus on being great at doing one thing instead of spreading yourself too thin by grasping for "bad revenue." www.smallgiantsbook.com.

READ NORM BRODSKY

Norm is a legend among entrepreneurs. He has started seven businesses and writes a column for *Inc.* magazine (back issues at www .inc.com).

SUBSCRIBE TO SMALL BUSINESS TRENDS

Anita Campbell is a multimedia maven of small business insight. She tweets, blogs, and writes to hundreds of thousands of small business owners each month. www.smallbiztrends.com.

READ *TOPGRADING* AND *TOPGRADING FOR SALES*

You'll learn about a great formula for hiring people, including the salespeople you'll need to drive your sales engine without you. www.smarttopgrading.com.

READ *BRAND: IT AIN'T THE LOGO*

Learn how to create a brand that is independent from you.

More resources and advice for creating a sellable business are available at www.BuiltToSell.com.